Reconciliation as Politics

CHURCH OF SWEDEN
Research Series

Göran Gunner, editor
Vulnerability, Churches and HIV (2009)

Kajsa Ahlstrand and Göran Gunner, editors
Non-Muslims in Muslim Majority Societies (2009)

Jonas Ideström, editor
For the Sake of the World (2010)

Göran Gunner and Kjell-Åke Nordquist
An Unlikely Dilemma (2011)

Anne-Louise Eriksson, Göran Gunner, and Niclas Blåder, editors
Exploring a Heritage (2012)

Kjell-Åke Nordquist, editor
Gods and Arms (2012)

Harald Hegstad
The Real Church (2013)

Carl-Henric Grenholm and Göran Gunner, editors
Justification in a Post-Christian Society (2014)

Carl-Henric Grenholm and Göran Gunner, editors
Lutheran Identity and Political Theology (2014)

Sune Fahlgren and Jonas Ideström, editors
Ecclesiology in the Trenches (2015)

Niclas Blåder
Lutheran Tradition as Heritage and Tool (2015)

Ulla Schmidt and Harald Askeland, editors
Church Reform and Leadership of Change (2016)

Kjell-Åke Nordquist
Reconciliation as Politics (2017)

Reconciliation as Politics
A Concept and Its Practice

KJELL-ÅKE NORDQUIST

☙PICKWICK *Publications* • Eugene, Oregon

RECONCILIATION AS POLITICS
A Concept and Its Practice

Church of Sweden Research Series 13

Copyright © 2017 Trossamfundet Svenska Kyrkan (Church of Sweden). All rights reserved. Except for brief quotations in critical publications or reviews, no part of this book may be reproduced in any manner without prior written permission from the publisher. Write: Permissions, Wipf and Stock Publishers, 199 W. 8th Ave., Suite 3, Eugene, OR 97401.

Pickwick Publications
An Imprint of Wipf and Stock Publishers
199 W. 8th Ave., Suite 3
Eugene, OR 97401

www.wipfandstock.com

PAPERBACK ISBN: 978-1-5326-0080-7
HARDCOVER ISBN: 978-1-5326-0082-1
EBOOK ISBN: 978-1-5326-0081-4

Cataloguing-in-Publication data:

Names: Nordquist, Kjell-Åke.

Title: Reconciliation as politics : a concept and its practice / Kjell-Åke Nordquist.

Description: Eugene, OR: Pickwick Publications, 2017 | Series: Church of Sweden Research Series | Includes bibliographical references.

Identifiers: ISBN 978-1-5326-0080-7 (paperback) | ISBN 978-1-5326-0082-1 (hardcover) | ISBN 978-1-5326-0081-4 (ebook)

Subjects: LSCH: Reconciliation—Political aspects.

Classification: JC580 N6 2017 (print) | JC580 (ebook)

Manufactured in the U.S.A.   08/25/17

Contents

List of Tables and Figures   vi
Preface   vii
Abbreviations   ix

1 Political Reconciliation—How Come?   1
2 Whose Truth and Which Reconciliation?   35
3 Five Ways of Dealing with the Past   46
4 A Structural Theory of Reconciliation   66
5 Human Rights and Peace-Building   77
6 Political Reconciliation and Human Rights—Matching or Not?   92
7 Legal Frameworks and International Peace   101
8 From East Timor to Timor Leste   107
9 A Reflection on Timor Leste   127
10 Political Reconciliation—A Contribution to Politics?   141

Appendix: Examples of Truth Commissions   151
Bibliography   161

List of Tables and Figures

Table 1. Four components in intra-state peace processes   8

Table 2. Four types of reconciliation settings and examples of cases   17

Table 3. Possible implications of Liberal and Communitarian perspectives on the truth concept   42

Table 4. Differences between conflict relation and reconciled relation   74

Table 5. Needs and providers of a peace structure   82

Table 6. Reconciliation debates on state/community level —examples of issues   90

Table 7. Experiences identifying human dignity   94

Table 8. Human dignity as a right and a gift   98

Table 9. Reconciliation and trust-building processes over time   140

Figure 1. Power relations, type of conflict, and four examples   20

Figure 2. The conflict triangle   24

Figure 3. A peace triangle   25

Figure 4. Four elements in a political reconciliation process   64

Figure 5. Four needs of security as a basis for peace-building   81

Figure 6. Three types of legal systems and their relations   105

Figure 7. Structural dividing lines in Timor Leste   129

Figure 8. Examples from Timor Leste of a comprehensive peace process   132

Figure 9. Vertical and horizontal reconciliation relations   138

Preface

The concept of reconciliation has made its way into political discourse and practice in recent decades. Is this an illustration of a deeper understanding on a global level of how life conditions are affected by conflict and war? Or is it the last straw in a world where stability and durable peace is too seldom the result of all the efforts in that direction? Most armed conflicts are internal to states, i.e., civil wars, and they are affecting populations often in a direct and protracted way, hurting normal civil life for years. Thus, the scale of negative impact and moral confusion resulting from civil wars is likely to be larger and more complex than in limited war situations with a controlled use of arms and soldiers. The settlement of such complex situations may require concepts that go beyond the traditional vocabulary of power, interests, and needs. It could be, that "reconciliation" also in politics serves the purpose of reaching beyond the traditional political language, into a sphere where politicians feel they have to contribute, but never had a language that was suitable for that.

For "reconciliation" the combination with truth—"truth and reconciliation"—is probably the most well known. The Truth and Reconciliation Commission in South Africa is globally well known along with some earlier and later commissions as well. Descriptions and analyzes of such commission's work are numerous and necessary parts of a development towards a more reflected and nuanced understanding of the phenomenon as such—"reconciliation in politics"—as well as its practice.

This book is however not yet another empirical or historical description of one or more truth and reconciliation commissions, or similar legal or political processes, but it is an attempt at approaching such processes from a reflection of the many dimensions that come along with bringing in "reconciliation" in the first place, into political processes. Its main focus is to deal with a simple question: does the concept of reconciliation bring anything "new" or useful to peace processes? From analyzing answers to that question we are in a position to reflect on the concept as such, examples of its practices, and on moral and ethical challenges that confront us in the midst of its application.

It is easy to assume, that what is understood on one level, in a certain cultural context, about "reconciliation" is also what the concept comes to represent on another level. It is not always or necessarily like that, but in addition to the complexity of the concept itself, one should never overlook the question whether there is a change in the understanding and application of what is labeled "reconciliation," when moving from being an interpersonal to become an intergroup and social concept.

While this study is not a purely conceptual one, it tries to focus on the conceptual ramifications that carry the idea of reconciliation in a political context forward in different settings. Thus, we will touch the transitional justice and the forgiveness debates, along with regular issues of peace and justice. However, as much as possible, we will stick to the line of political reconciliation and try to give an account on its own terms and resources.

The texts in this book are based on experiences from a combination of research and field work carried out mainly in South East Asia (East Timor/Timor Leste) and Australia, in Latin America (mainly Colombia) and in the Middle East (Israel and Palestine) during a period of about two decades. To research institutions and diplomatic missions, to individual scholars and friends, to actors taking their duties serious in our negotiations and meetings, and to numerous individuals who shared their reflections and life stories on "political reconciliation"—to all, I would like to express a warm word of gratitude.

Kjell-Åke Nordquist
Uppsala, December 2016

Abbreviations

AIETD	All Inclusive Intra-East Timorese Dialogue
Apodeti	Timorese Popular Democratic Association
ASDT	Timorese Association of Social Democrats
AUC	United Self-Defense Forces of Colombia
BRTT	East Timor People's Front
CAVR	Commission for Reception, Truth and Reconciliation
CNRM	National Council of Maubere Resistance
CNRT	National Council of Timorese Resistance
CTF	Commission of Truth and Friendship Indonesia-Timor Leste
ETSG	East Timor Study Group
Falintil	National Liberation Forces of East Timor
FARC	Revolutionary Armed Forces of Colombia
Fretilin	Revolutionary Front for an Independent East Timor
ICC	International Criminal Court
Interfet	International Force East Timor
LRA	Lord's Resistance Army
LTTE	Liberation Tigers of Tamil Eelam
NGO	Non-governmental organization
OECD	Organisation for Economic Co-operation and Development
UN	United Nations
UNTAET	United Nations Transitional Administration for East Timor
TNI	Indonesian Armed Forces
TRC	South African Truth and Reconciliation Commission
UDT	Timorese Democratic Union

1

Political Reconciliation—How Come?

The question is simple: is the concept of "reconciliation" a substantial contribution to the form and content of peace processes after armed conflict and war? One may ask why the question is of interest in the first place, but the concept has gradually entered into the national and international political discourse on peace issues since more than three decades. Such a development is likely to reflect at least some dimensions of theoretical interest. The concept's main context has been in connection to the ending of authoritarian rule or civil wars and as a bridging metaphor for necessary social changes in the construction of peace and new political structures.

Every such conceptual change of context is interesting, because something happens to the content of a concept when it changes environment, and is interpreted and used by persons in roles very different from the traditional roles connected to the concept. From psychotherapy, religion, and casual talk about life and death, the concept of "reconciliation" has made its way into speeches by prime ministers and representatives of global international organizations, sometimes with the addition of "political." The impression today is, that there is no major political statement about justice, war, and peace, which does not also refer to a process with the final goal of "reconciliation."

This development is interesting not only from a political science point of view, but from a wider social science and cultural perspective: the conceptual landscape which accompanies the usage of "reconciliation" includes a number of other concepts as well, such as "truth," "reparation," "justice," "pardon," and "peace." The introduction of "reconciliation" brings also a context of perceptions and perspectives that refer not only to the empirical world, but also to a sense of "purpose," of "direction," and of a view of life as "meaningful," or something that should be lived in dignity. All these are concepts that each one of them raises fundamental philosophical and political questions. Over a few decades only, they have become part of a political vocabulary when talking about peace, politics, and society.

The purpose of this book is however more than only observing a change of concepts in a political language. A key question in this investigation is: in what way, if any, does "political reconciliation" enrich and promote processes towards conflict resolution and peace? Do we see in this concept just another twist of words, in the seemingly ever-expanding market of policy-nurturing ideas? In addition to these questions we may as well discuss the reasons behind this development, for instance if the introduction of "political reconciliation" relates to the changing landscape of armed conflicts: from interstate war to internal armed conflict, or to changing relations between the state and its subjects in the same period.

Thus we are interested in both the concept as such, and the consequences of its implementation in peace processes.

HUMAN RIGHTS—A GLOBAL RESPONSIBILITY

A major achievement of the twentieth century was the creation of internationally binding legal instruments that bring the individual person into the realm of international, and not only national, commitments. When the ideas and concepts of human rights were formulated in the Universal Declaration of Human Rights in 1948, they were thought of as internal responsibilities for states, the international state-border was an absolute limit for any other state wishing to meddle into internal affairs of other states. Today there is however a wide recognition of an international responsibility for instance when it comes to protect populations from crimes committed by their own leaders. The principle of Responsibility to Protect is presently the most codified, but also the most debated, example of this fundamental change of states' views upon each other.[1]

---

1. The United Nations General Assembly endorsed in 2005 a resolution based on the connection between sovereignty of a state and its capacity to protect its own population against serious crimes, such as ethnic cleansing, crimes against humanity, genocide and war crimes. Failure by a state to protect its own population in this respect gives a responsibility to the international community to do so instead, through a set of measures, including armed intervention.

Not only states came to be holders of rights and duties at the end of the last century, but also individual persons—whether in private capacity or (even) as state servants. It was a process that took shape in different ways. A milestone in that development, after the Universal Declaration of Human Rights, is the establishment of the International Criminal Court, (ICC), based on the Rome Statute from 1998. These two mechanisms—so different in nature but with the same basic idea of defending fundamental dignity and human rights—combine the fact that individuals, besides states, have both rights and duties which do not limit themselves to, for instance, state boundaries or professional roles. Thus they are applicable not only in civil life but also under the special legal and practical conditions that define a situation of armed conflict and war. This is our *first* observation of the changing normative conditions since the last century, for peace processes and for politics in general, on the global level.

FROM INTERSTATE TO INTRASTATE ARMED CONFLICTS

While these are developments within the human rights sphere, there is a *second* important change after the Second World War: armed conflicts and wars have gradually turned into a blend of internal and inter-state conflict. The typical, history-book type of interstate war is a rare event, and during some years in the last decades there has been no such war in the conflict statistics at all.[2] On the surface this was not always visible: the Cold War was a period where some conflict areas were fuelled while others were kept under control. Only a few conflicts were inter-state conflicts, such as India-Pakistan, Ecuador-Perú, and Iran-Iraq.

As a systematic collection of data shows, the totally dominating number of wars are, since decades back, "internal wars." They are either about the political control of a given state ("civil war") or about a state's fundamental structure as a state, in practice often a claim of autonomy or secession ("state formation conflict"). *Civil wars* are thus challenging an existing government, its policy etc. but not the state as a unit, while *state formation conflicts* are doing just that.[3] They include issues which one or more of the

2. Pettersson and Wallensteen, "Armed Conflicts."

3. "War" and "armed conflict" is here used without distinction. In conflict statistics "wars" are often defined as armed conflicts with 1000 or more battle-related deaths per year, while an "armed conflict," or "major armed conflict," has less numbers of fatalities per year. See also Pettersson and Wallensteen, "Armed Conflicts."

parties pursue as means to change the state itself. Some may want local autonomy or other forms for self-rule and others want to go further. The most radical type of proposals is that about a territorial separation and independence of regions within states. Such demands for secession have been on the agenda for armed groups in Europe as well as in Africa and Asia. Colombia, Sierra Leone, and Afghanistan are examples of countries with civil wars, and the conflicts in Southern Sudan, Sri Lanka, Northern Ireland, Spain (the Basque conflict), and the Philippines (Mindanao) are historic and ongoing examples of countries with state formation conflicts.

While internal wars dominate as the typical armed conflict of today, they have at the same time become *internationalized*. This is kind of a half-way return to the inter-state battle, but within the framework and disguise of a civil war and not seldom as part of a multi-lateral struggle between states on the soil of a third state—if a state intervenes in a neighbor's territory, other neighbors tend to do the same. This phenomenon is obviously likely to contribute to the protraction of civil wars. It can be regarded as an expansion of a "horizontal" dimension of civil wars. The Democratic Republic of Congo has for many years been a prominent example of this type of conflict.

Civil wars imply also a "vertical" dimension of fragmentation: they are gradually digging into all spheres of life in a state. The national leadership is challenged through the increased role of powerful layers after layers of informal practices taking over decision-making, for instance in local administrations of states. This process is often parallel to the same fragmentation of control of the army and of security forces in general. This sort of development has as one consequence that large portions of a population become seriously affected by war, much larger than would be the case, for instance, if the conflict was fought by regular troops in limited geographical areas. Consequently, protracted civil wars are particularly devastating for the civil population. They are major producers of wide streams of refugees today.

This is however not the end of a disappointing development. Sometimes the grim effect of civil war is turned into a strategy of the parties—if there is no enemy army to fight, for whatever reason, the civilian population can very well in itself be a target. This can be so for many reasons: the population is in a classic guerilla strategy the basis for its own guerilla forces, and therefore it is the enemy's protection, in the view of the opposing side. A second reason can be material, populations represent capacity and competence which can be a support for one side or the other, and, third, the population can represent the identity of the enemy and is therefore not only a symbol, but the actual carrier of values and culture. In such instances, rape, genocide, and systematic killing of groups, or of whole populations, become tempting strategic goals from a military and ideological point of view. This is where we find examples of the most serious crimes of war that the international community is aware of, such as crimes against humanity. The result of all this is that displacement, killing, and human suffering on the whole is most severe among civilians in modern armed conflicts.

This has obviously consequences for a peace process. It is not far away to conclude—given the broad negative effects of civil wars—that *if the war affects everyone, also the peace process should include everyone.* This should be so for moral reasons, but also from strategic: it makes sense to assume that peace—on all levels of a society—is more likely to be established if all levels of a society also have been addressed and included in a peace process—from participation to compensation and redefining the structures and policies of a new society.

BLURRED BOUNDARY BETWEEN WAR TYPES

A *third* observation of changes is a consequence of what we noted above, about the changing nature of most armed conflicts and wars. The classical "declaration of war" that used to be made at the early stage of interstate war fighting, meant that the rules and responsibilities of soldiers were from that moment of a military, and not civilian, nature. The declaration was also a sign to neutral states, that their neutralization was now a valid and respected position in the view of the war fighting states. Since actors in a civil war, almost by definition, benefit from surprise, low-level fighting and infiltration, a declaration of war is from this point of view counterproductive, it is an impractical and seemingly irrelevant act.

The nature of civil war is part of the puzzle: civil war means in practice fighting "by civilians, among civilians." This has blurred the line between war and peace from a legal point of view and also blurred the respect for rules that belong to situations of "war" or of "peace." The unclear situation is underlined but the fact that in many countries, the difference between armed criminal violence and regular guerilla fights is difficult to distinguish. This is particularly true in situations where guerilla movements, besides their traditional and purported role as politically motivated fighters, for financial reasons also involve in kidnappings, murder, and extortion, just like any criminal band.

The human loss and suffering, together with the physical and environmental destruction after a civil war creates on the whole a situation of such a magnitude, that it goes far beyond the capacity of any normally functioning state would have at its disposal to deal with; so much less then, for a state in a post-conflict situation with a history of many years, maybe decades, of fighting. This leads to very uncomfortable decisions regarding the priority order of using scarce resources, both material and human, and its short- and long-term effects on the development of a country.

The three tendencies noted above, points in a direction where what is individual and what is political come closer to each other. The codification of human dignity through universal human rights, on the one hand, and the dominating trend of armed conflicts to be internal, has created a somewhat paradoxical situation in many countries, where the dignity of the individual is strengthened on paper but weakened in real life. This has happened while at the same time, the threats to human dignity on a general and global scale have undergone a change as well—from oppression, poverty and armed conflict to also include environmental change, global criminal activity, and trade with both humans and human organs.

The need for reconciliation in a political context can always be discussed. What is a manageable deficiency in a society, something that can be the case without anyone's intention, may not produce effects that motivate a reconciliation process in the same way as a long-term and direct infringement of a person's human rights might do. At this point it is however necessary to be alert: what at one point in time is seen as a "manageable deficiency" can in another time period or context be regarded as a serious violation. Each historic time, and each society, has probably its own reasons for restoring dignity of individuals or groups.

The typical situation discussed in this book is that a political agenda, whether from the government or an opposition group, has been promoted in a way (military dictatorship or armed conflict) that has infringed on the integrity and dignity of an individual person. Given that this broader scope of responsibility is acknowledged, the instruments by which "peace" is established expand from the classical two-state peace agreement to mechanisms which include legal and moral means, both individual and collective.

As a way of dealing with such a broad challenge, peace processes have taken on wider responsibilities in the last decades. This has been possible to an increasing extent in particular since the end of the Cold War, in the 1990s. Individual peace processes may have looked different, and developed different aspects of a wide spectrum of mechanisms and dimensions that actually might be part of a process. Table 1 below is an attempt at summarizing four main components in what could be called a "comprehensive peace process":

- the formal peace agreement,
- a process of individual legal responsibility,
- apologies by state or other leaders, and
- a mechanism, such as truth and reconciliation commissions.

These four aspects of peace are very often found in ongoing peace processes, but not necessarily at the same time. Rather, that would most likely cause new problems of coordination and mandate. While most of the components have been commented on above, the apology aspect has not. It refers to the many cases of apologies expressed by Heads of state, leaders of parties or international organizations, churches, etc. who apologize to victimized groups—for instance after civil wars or with regards to historically victimized groups, including indigenous peoples.[4] In the following of this book, this dimension together with the truth dimension, will be the two ones most analyzed and developed.

A COMPREHENSIVE PEACE PROCESS

Few peace processes, if any, can at the same time realize all four components illustrated in Table 1. It is not even obvious if it is desirable that they appear simultaneously. For instance, an apology is not a time consuming act in itself, but it may have an impact on the quality of other processes. Legal processes, on the other hand, are time-consuming. One thing is sure: the timing of the four parts will impact on the process and we have little understanding of how they *de facto* relate to each other. So far only one relationship has been discussed on the basis of observed conflicts of interest, and that is the issue

---

4. For instance, when traveling in Africa and Rwanda, UN Secretary-General Kofi Annan apologized for the UN inability to protect the Rwandans from the genocide; Queen Elizabeth of United Kingdom has apologized for British exploitation of the Maoris; the Japanese Prime Minister has apologized for what the country did in China, Korea, and the Philippines during the Second World War.

to what extent witnessing for a truth commission shall be, or not be, possible to contribute to a legal process—whether parallel or held later.

Table 1. Four components in intra-state peace processes

	Political level	Individual level
Legal aspect	Formal peace agreement	Responsibility according to national/international law; War Crime Tribunals
Moral aspect	Apology from leaders	Truth and reconciliation commissions

If we regard a *peace process* as—ideally—containing all these four possible dimensions, the *political reconciliation process,* in the widest sense of the concept, should be seen as supported by all these aspects. The reconciliation dimension is then included in each part of this comprehensive peace process, rather than being a last resort if there is a failure in one or many of the specific parts of the process.

So, back to our introductory question about the contribution of "political reconciliation." Let's use the concept of "truth" as a tool for identifying the nature of such a contribution. Table 1 indicates, that mechanisms are there, available to deal with the impact of civil wars in societies. At best, the four components in a process could strengthen each other, be complementary and add to each other's legitimacy. For this reason, the reconciliation process, should not be used as a remedy for failures in the other squares of the table, but rather be seen as an integrative part of a larger whole.

If we come back to the aspect of timing, the *formal peace agreement,* many would say, should be the start. However, also an *apology* from responsible leaders should be an early initiative. If so it would be a trigger towards an agreement, including a larger peace process, and thus serve a specific purpose at an early stage. Whether legal and reconciliatory processes should overlap in time or not, is often a matter due to the relationship between the two. A well-known example of the tension this can cause is Sierra Leone, where there was a sharp disagreement between the National Truth and Reconciliation Commission, and the international Special Court set up for dealing with crimes against humanity in the war.[5] This tension was partly due to the Court's over-ruling of some of the conditions in the peace agreement. The challenge is then to design a reconciliation process that integrates with other parts of the peace process, and thereby becomes a process in its own right.

In order to answer the introductory question—political reconciliation—how come?—the nature of today's armed conflicts is closest to an explanation: as internal wars are affecting wide groups of populations and they require for this reason another form of moral and individual treatment than what history books used to say about inter-state peace agreements and peace processes. As we have seen, there are mechanisms available; experiences are made in a number of countries and processes, dealing with different ways and means of dealing with the past, often with a reconciliation dimension involved.

RECONCILIATION IN POLITICS

The phenomenon of "reconciliation" does take place in real life, between individuals and between groups, but does this fact make it a something that could be useful in what we call "politics"? Not necessarily, of course. Politics, as it is usually understood, deals with power, that is, the distribution of resources—in an ever-changing society. It is for many an important principle that certain aspects of life should stay out of influence of "politics." Is maybe reconciliation also such a concept?

There are two observations to be made in relation to this. The first is, that when it comes to peace processes after civil war, and in particular after protracted civil wars, we do not only talk about a political process in the narrow sense, meaning a process that depends solely on actions from governments or political leaders. Peace processes after civil wars are wider than so. They are social processes, which encompass much broader layers of a society than are usually influenced by governmental structures. So for that reason, reconciliation can at least in principle have a place in a peace process understood in this wider sense. If we have a *wide* definition of "peace," then it is not difficult to see how reconciliation can be part of a wide definition of a wide peace process.

The other observation is, that as much as reconciliation depends on the free will of people to change their attitudes and insights, its scope and

---

5. For an overview of truth commissions see Appendix.

RECONCILIATION AS POLITICS

pace will always be individually decided, it can never be commanded by political decision. Governments and governmental agencies can provide space and opportunity for reconciliation to take place, but not so much more, really. They should not press individuals to actions beyond what is felt as appropriate—morally and politically—by the individual person. In addition to this, it should always be remembered, that this is all about situations where many persons are deeply victimized. Who is to tell, under such conditions, that a change of mind shall take place, and who is to ask if it can happen "now"?

RECONCILIATION—A NOTE ON THE CULTURAL QUESTION

The conceptual overlapping between "reconciliation" and for instance Christian teaching about mercy, forgiveness, and reconciliation—doesn't it make reconciliation also in politics part of a Western agenda, part of a Western cultural dominance, when introduced in politics in non-Western societies and cultures? That question is legitimate but it should not put us into the assumption that there are no social practices that in form and content resemble more or less of what the English concept of reconciliation stands for.[6] The conceptual variety that exists, and its different translations, plus the shifting phenomenological meanings that are reflected in these expressions obviously create a "risk" for a plural understanding of the phenomenon that we all try to understand. In practice, a continued communication about the concept and its practices, normally creates a common operational understanding of what is meant by "reconciliation" or "political reconciliation." That holds very far.

The theoretical problem raised by cultural differences should not be, and is not, an absolute barrier to meaningful cross-cultural reflection and analysis about what in English is labeled "political reconciliation." The critical aspect in a theoretical context is whether "reconciliation" represents a social phenomenon that is universal or not in character. If so, this phenomenon is the center of the dialogue, not the more or less overlapping concepts used to describe it. Tools can always be better in relation to their task, and it is important that we understand this problem in this way: first the phenomenon, than the conceptual tool.

---

6. For many examples, see Malley-Morrison et al., *International Handbook*.

SOME OBSERVATIONS FROM THE LITERATURE

When a new field of research emerges, in this case alongside with a number of early examples of the phenomenon to be studied, case studies and studies of principle and conceptual focus are dominating. This is true also for the research on aspects of reconciliation in a political context, and some of these studies are referred to in this study. A signal of a certain amount of relevant studies is the publication of the "handbook," something that in social sciences indicates an ambition to cover more or less all essential dimensions within a field.[7]

For the purpose of this study, the scholarly debate about "political reconciliation" that is of most interest, contains basically two main strands, a secular "liberal peace" approach and a "religion-based" approach, where the latter focuses on relation-building based on the concepts of justice and recognition.

The *liberal agenda* looks with skepticism to political reconciliation since the concept seems too soft, or too wide, to be able to contribute to a "concept family" based on democracy, rule of law, human rights, accountability, and international law. These concepts are, in liberal peace thinking, holding together in a system of principles and rules that apply from a principled approach to peace negotiations, for instance in relation to the rule of law and legal processes for dealing with violations and crimes against international law during conflict. This is the most important contribution of the liberal peace agenda in a post-conflict context besides the introduction of the democratic political system, including its components of elections and a constitution built on democratic norms and practices.

Through the introduction of democratic norms and practices, such as elections, rule of law and an accountable administrative system, a society in transition from war to peace will have the best possible basis for its recovery from its historic ordeal. The role of the international community is, in line with this view, defined by these democracy-centered concepts—to introduce and institutionalize them is the responsibility that the international system has, and it is normally a goal of its interventions and missions.

An alternative agenda of political reconciliation claims that *relation-building* is the key purpose of political reconciliation and is therefore to some extent critical to the liberal agenda, which is seen as too limited. According to this view, the liberal agenda's concepts and practices are too

---

7. A good example is ibid.

limited to deal effectively with such a profound experience and redefinition of a society that comes out as a necessary consequence of a civil war. Therefore, it is no wonder that international panels and courts are weak in following up the rights of victims (to compensation, for instance). Also the multitudes of truth perceptions and the right for any society to use its cultural norms and practices as part of dealing with one's own history are dimensions that the liberal peace has difficulties to deal with.

While the liberal agenda is focusing on the individual's rights and duties, and on the society's duty to exact justice and conform to international norms of justice and human rights in post-conflict situations, the relation-building agenda would claim that the relation-building capacity of democracy and human rights are strong qualities, that should be both respected and utilized for peace-building, but nevertheless, they are too limited to grasp the cornerstones for their own utility: basic trust, the respect for human imperfection and understanding of a shared fate. Without an understanding of such factors, democracy and justice will not be able to come into reality in the first place.

Daniel Philpott, for instance, argues that armed conflict and wars harm persons—irrespective of side in a conflict—in totally six ways and they are all are examples of political injustices: violation of human rights, secondary effects of such harms (trauma, losses of loved ones, etc.), ignorance of the source of harm, non-recognition of suffering, the "standing victory" proclaimed if the perpetrator "wins," and the wounds inflicted on the perpetrator from violent acts.[8] These fundamental injustices are deep scars in a society and therefore reflecting what reconciliation, as a peace-building concept, should deal with.

While not in any sense mechanically mirroring the six injustices, Philpott constructs an understanding of political reconciliation as a concept of justice, where its "animating virtue is mercy and its goal is peace."[9] "Political reconciliation," then, becomes an umbrella concept for a set of conditions which together work as a remedy against political injustices, namely a just government, acknowledgement, reparation, punishment, apology, and forgiveness. This gives "reconciliation" a less active role than the other concepts, it becomes dependent on them and does not in itself introduce any (new) quality to the political process, besides the framing of a number of parameters in a reconciliation context, and the

8. Philpott, *Just and Unjust Peace*.
9. Philpott, "An Ethic of Political," 390.

identification of their concerted contribution to a social change, which then is called "reconciliation."

In this way Philpott avoids the problem created by the unclear boundaries between, for instance, the concepts of forgiveness and reconciliation. At the same time, the possible contribution of "reconciliation" is set aside for a role as a concept of justice, which in practice means, for instance, that the qualities that makes it distinct from forgiveness, are not really given a chance to contribute in a concrete political process.

Andrew Schaap calibrates his concept of "political reconciliation" between an understanding of Charles Taylor's concepts of recognition and identity and Frantz Fanon's position that recognition is basically about power in a context (of a subject-object-relationship) and therefore oppressive by definition. The "fusion of horizons" which Taylor hopes for, as a basis for reconciliation, is neither possible nor preferable for Fanon, who argues that reconciliation is possible on the basis of non-recognition from an agonistic point of view. Any society, any community "is always not yet," according to Schaap and therefore it would benefit from living in an open relation to other communities. It is simply not necessary to create a common identity, based on previous antagonistic relations between groups or individuals. Rather, according to Schaap, political reconciliation should "depend on founding and sustaining a space for politics within which the emergence of a common identity is an ever present possibility."[10]

A THIN AND THICK RECONCILIATION

Schaap's understanding of political reconciliation can be described as "thin," and Philpott's as "thick." "Thin" because it waters out the existential dimensions of conflict for the individual and the society's need for institutional confidence-building in situations of fundamental insecurity and uncertainty. For the purpose of avoiding the risk of jumping into the recognition corner, actions of great importance to groups or individuals are likely to be withheld with a strong application of a "thin" political reconciliation of this type.

On the other hand, a "thick" response to the same situation is so full of (proposed) practices to correct injustice that some of their internal relationships are neither clarified theoretically, nor explained in terms of effectiveness in relation to the goal of creating peace.

10. Schaap, "Political Reconciliation," 538.

RECONCILIATION AS POLITICS

The victim's role and potential as a contributor to a new society is not explicitly recognized in Philpott's list. At best it is a consequence of the many practices, but from them do not necessarily follow a strengthening of a person's agency or relations. While relation-building is key in Philpott's proposal, there is only one relationship-building practice in the list: forgiveness, and this is not a "simple" concept to deal with in this context, and not the most natural one for creating relations.

It is understandable that this is the case, since reconciliation is by nature concerned with the past in many ways, but its purpose, as Philpott rightly says, its goal is peace—a futural concept.

Actually all practices, to a smaller or greater extent, in Philpott's list are of a unilateral nature. Almost all reflect asymmetric relations. The victim of injustice is a receiver of apology, of its oppressor's punishment, reparation, acknowledgement, and human rights in a just society. The vision of active participation in, and if necessary re-introduction to, the life of a community which has been a threat for a long period is an important dimension in political reconciliation—it would not deserve to be named political without a specific reference to the community, of course.

In the end of Philpott's list, the victim may be asked to forgive. It is correct that such an act can strengthen the agency of the person, when introduced by the victim and on the conditions of the victim. However, as will be argued later, forgiveness as a concept has unique qualities and is therefore, it can be argued, not a politically useful concept. The fact that it is surrounded by many qualifications, when used in a political context, testifies to this.

From the positions taken by Philpott and Schaap, respectively, it seems advisable to identify an understanding of "political reconciliation" that is "thick enough" to provide substantial content to victims and their societies in times of post-conflict and rebuilding societies, on the one hand, and "thin enough" to allow for tensions to remain in the political arena, and be expressed as genuine expressions of needs, identity, and interests—that is, without trying to settle finally, what can never be finally settled.

RECONCILIATION—BOTH A GOAL AND A PROCESS

Obviously, "reconciliation" represents a *process* as well as a *goal* for that same process. As a process it refers both to political, social, and legal components, and it has in practice come to include the acknowledgement of victims, truth telling, reparation, and justice. The relation between these components can of course be discussed. For some groups, "justice," "truth," or "reparation" are all a *sine qua non* for reconciliation. It is however possible to develop a position, as is seen below, that political reconciliation is not a mere composition of aspects, but has a distinct meaning and contribution in itself, to the nature of peace processes, besides these other concepts.

As a *goal*, there are two types of reconciliation that need to be identified; both are relevant for protracted armed conflicts. The first and most common is *intra*-generational political reconciliation, i.e., a process between persons who themselves have experienced, or for that matter, committed, atrocities, in short: those that have suffered and carried the burdens related to that suffering—victims and perpetrators alike.

In *inter*-generational reconciliation processes, however, we deal with those individuals and groups who have to come to grips with prejudices and memories, and who have had to grow up in divided communities, due to past grievances and divisions. Here, dealing with history, so that it in itself does not become a new reason for conflict, is a major challenge—for individuals as well as societies.

There are some distinctive features of these two types. A fundamental observation about inter-generational reconciliation is that while being a victim easily translates into the second generation, both in terms of perceptions and world-views, as well as materially, the same does however not as easily apply to perpetrators. From a legal point this is obvious, but also morally, the responsibility looks different—from culture to culture—when it comes to compensating in one way or another for what "our fathers did."

Many countries have struggled with inter-generational reconciliation, for example Germany and Poland, Germany and France, Japan and its South-East Asian neighbors, and Spain, to take a few examples. These processes have included everything from leaders' pronouncements and apologies for the past, to common history book projects. Such a long-term process of a conscious re-building of understanding and acceptance of a common fate and history is an interesting and important investment in time and effort. It is more difficult to measure its effect or impact over time, but as often in similar cases, it may not be the result in itself that is the most important aspect, but the process—with all its reassessments, acknowledgements, and new insights on all sides involved.

In countries which have experienced protracted armed conflicts, such as India and Pakistan, Burma/Myanmar, Israel and Palestine, and

RECONCILIATION AS POLITICS

Colombia, and maybe a few more, experiences from inter-generational reconciliation processes could provide important issues to be considered, if and when these areas and countries are abound for reconciliation on a national, political level.

We should here also note, that there is a growing literature on the question of "historic responsibility," i.e., if subsequent generations have the moral obligation to meet demands of reparation for injustices carried out by previous generations, for instance towards indigenous peoples, slaves, colonial peoples, etc.[11]

FOUR RECONCILIATION CONTEXTS

The distinction between inter- and intra-generational reconciliation has been mentioned briefly already. There are obviously a number of practical issues connected to this difference, but it raises also some fundamental ethical and philosophical issues, related to the degree of responsibility—if any—that can be transferred between generations, and as a corollary: can victimization be inherited, and if so, in what way? This is a major issue for political actors as well as philosophers.[12]

All of these issues are in various ways already dealt with in daily life as well as in our conceptions of what it means to live—in relation to morality, responsibility, and how injustice is dealt with.

Some empirical cases are likely to represent mainly one of these four categories of reconciliation; this is illustrated in Table 2.

---

11. For a study arguing for trans-generational responsibilities, see Thompson, *Taking Responsibility*.

12. For an overview of such issues, see ibid.

Table 2. Four types of reconciliation settings and examples of cases

	Intra-generational	Inter-generational
Largely one-sided violations (one side is a victim, other side perpetrator)	Genocide; Massacres; Oppression	Systems of segregation; Racial laws
Largely two-sided violations (both sides have inflicted grave injustices on each other)	Armed conflicts/wars	Protracted armed conflicts/wars

Besides this time-based distinction of reconciliation contexts, another distinction of fundamental importance is the nature of the relationship between the victim and the perpetrators: are victims always "only" victims, and are perpetrators always "only" perpetrators? It is not a surprise that individuals or groups, that may very well be regarded as victims from one point of view, also have been in situations where they have inflicted harm upon the other side.

Obviously there are specific situations where it is possible to make such a black-and-white distinction on good grounds. However, there are probably other and more cases where the dominating impression in terms of "who is who?" is more "grey," they have different moral shades. However, there are also many clear examples of a dominating relationship between victim and perpetrator. In many cases it can be distinguished between a unilateral and a mixed moral relationship between the victim and perpetrator, i. e. between a "unilateral victimhood" and a "reciprocal victimhood." The exceptions to the rule do not rule out the distinction as such, something which is important for how the two sides can relate to each other in a coming political reconciliation process. This is a major issue, a very sensitive issue, in situations where the victim becomes the power holder as an outcome of the process, such as in the case of South Africa, Timor Leste, Bosnia-Herzegovina, and Sierra Leone.

With these observations as a background—what does it mean to political reconciliation with such different structural conditions? An hypothesis we can formulate, and which we can bring further into the discussion later, is that the closer in time, and the more distinct separation of groups in terms of acts and motives, the more instrumental forms for reconciliation are likely to be effective. These can vary, from legal processes, to short-term and intensive national reconciliation programs, to unilateral acts of repentance, or apologies. In line with this, we would then also assume that the longer conflict process in time, the more people are involved and therefore the moral diversity among victims and perpetrators is likely to be greater than otherwise. Therefore we are likely to assume that reconciliation, political as well as on an even broader social scale, to be more durable if it takes place in forms that represent such a moral diversity. In the end, for very long-term and deep conflict histories, maybe only a nation's culture can be such a multi-scalar reconciliation mechanism that reaches beyond legal processes and political apologies—from traditional historic forms of literature, music and dancing to more recently developed cultural expressions through digital media and a globalized consciousness.

THE POWER DIMENSION

There is a fundamental difference for any legal or reconciliatory process—or peace process on the whole for that matter—if the parties have agreed to the process as a result of *negotiation* where no side has been forced to give up militarily, and a situation where one of the sides on good grounds can claim *military victory* over the other, and therefore in practice can impose not only the negotiations as such but often also the outcome of these negotiations. However, this is not equal to a totally asymmetric situation. It is not so, that the loosing side does not have bargaining power, its support may still be widespread and influential.

An agreement, negotiated without imposition between two parties, recognizes that the two sides have a capacity strong enough to destroy an agreement, should there be one. Nevertheless the parties have agreed to settle their differences through negotiations, for reasons that the rest of us can guess, and only they themselves can fully explain. Such processes are often marred with political argument, deception, maneuvers, broken cease-fires, and the like. Still, the leadership on both/all sides can be very clear in the intention.

It should be remembered here that, for instance, in the South African process towards a post-apartheid democratic state in the 1990s, there was never a formal cease-fire signed between the involved parties. Nevertheless, the course of events was clear, even when it was challenged in substance and practice by many groups and events at the time. While its was clear in South Africa that the days of the apartheid system were counted, and from this point the case of South Africa seems less of a negotiated process, there was still a lot of political space in that process, used by all parties. This was so also in relation to the constitutional process.

Another case in point of negotiated peace processes is Colombia, and, for instance the demobilization process of the right-wing paramilitary groups under the United Self-Defense Forces of Colombia (AUC) between 2004 and 2006. The paramilitaries tried, by showing good will and good intentions through participating in demobilization programs, to get a favorable position in the final balance of accountability vis-à-vis the state.[13] This did not materialize, however. The AUC was by the international community listed as a terrorist organization and were facing justice in Colombia through a legal process defined by Law 975. The outcome of the whole process was romped, since all major leaders were extradited to the United States in 2008, on drug charges.

The negotiations in Cuba between the Colombian government and the largest leftist guerilla group, The Revolutionary Armed Forces of Colombia (FARC), is a typical case of a negotiated settlement, where both sides have the resources to continue the conflict but for various reasons have decided not to continue the violent way. This means in practice that compromises are made within a wide range of areas, and no one will come out as a victor—or maybe, both will present themselves as the victors. A critical point is the political future of FARC, something that was agreed upon as possible in the final agreement.

The case of Rwanda is different. There was—and is—a heavy moral burden on the perpetrators of the genocide, but from a democratic point of view, this burden cannot imply that there is, or there shall not be, any room for other actors or opinions in the society, than the dominating one. The same is true for East Timor, where the winning side, and its subsequent governments, won a victory so strong that the political space of the side that lost the referendum about the future of East Timor, faces the risk of being reduced only because it had a clear minority outcome in the referendum.[14]

---

13. Nordquist and Koonings, *Peace Processes*.

14. The winning, pro-independence option in the referendum on East Timor's future status got 78.5 percent of the votes, while the pro-autonomy (within Indonesia) option got 21.5 percent.

RECONCILIATION AS POLITICS

This is a general problem, and illustrates the power dimension, something that of course is typical for politics. However, the idea behind for instance democratic institutions is to hinder one group's monopolization of political life and mechanisms. This is the issue of concern also in a political reconciliation process.

Before we close the discussion on power, we also need to take into account the nature of social situations where political reconciliation has been considered. The main ideas behind the concept of "political reconciliation," together with "transitional justice," grew out of the dissolution of the military dictatorships in Latin America in the 1980s and subsequent commissions in the region. These became a template for the more well-known South African Truth and Reconciliation Commission in 1995. The critical issue was about how to deal with the legitimate claim for justice and the rights of victims, on the one hand, and, on the other, maintain stability in a society where the perpetrators and the institutions they represent, are still powerful forces. With military control of government at the time, the economic power-holders were safe in their control of resources, and democracy was a secondary thing for them, in relation to that interest. There were large numbers of persons killed, disappeared etc. but there was not an open armed fight as in a guerilla war. Forms of resistance under oppression can vary over time and the line between these two is not clear cut. However, four countries are nevertheless good examples of very different situations—all of which have been part of discussions about political reconciliation.

Figure 1. Power relations, type of conflict, and four examples

```
                    Mixed "victory"
                          ↑
           Chile          |       Colombia
                          |
                          |                Liberation/
    Elite control  ←——————+——————→         guerilla movements
                          |
         El Salvador      |       South Africa
                          ↓
                   One-sided "victory"
```

Political Reconciliation—How Come?

We are now ready for combining the "degree of victory," that is the power balance between the parties when they negotiate, and the nature of the conflict that they have been fighting. In order to make clear the different conditions under which reconciliation processes take place, Figure 1 describes these four examples.

In the context of reconciliation, we need to recognize that since reconciliation by nature is a voluntary process—which is different from legal processes for instance—the power dimension will play a strong role for its success. This leads naturally over to the next problem—what to do in a still violent context?

RECONCILIATION IN A VIOLENT CONTEXT

Obviously, "reconciliation" in the midst of ongoing violence—both in a concrete, almost geographical sense, and/or politically—faces the risk of becoming a distorted version of its intentions. Shall enemies reconcile over the weekend and renew their fighting on Monday? This is of course the opposite of any reconciliation idea. The critical question is here: Under what circumstances can reconciliation be initiated as an effective[15] part of a peace process?

One bottom-line would be to say, that for an effective reconciliation process, it should be safeguarded from being kidnapped for partisan political purposes. If the purpose of political reconciliation is to overcome divisions, then the process needs to stand above the divisions themselves. This principle is in a way obvious, maybe simplistic, but it addresses not only issues in the formation of a process, such as the choice of leading personalities, but also staffing and financial and other practical aspects as well.

More intriguing is the issue of political conditions for a reconciliation process. A tentative conclusion, given the experiences from truth and reconciliation commissions from three decades, is that the higher level of ongoing violence during the work of the commission—with or without a final peace accord signed—the more shallow or limited work of the commission. Violence always limits the work of a truth commission: its political support, its witnesses, its possibility to move, the security for its members, etc. In order for a commission to work effectively, in the midst of ongoing violence, a possible approach would be to structure the work into units of a geographical and political nature. For instance, in regions

---

15. "Effective" is here standing for "meaningful," "relevant," and "productive."

where demobilization has taken place, and where leaders signal willingness to redefine their position, a reconciliation process can be contemplated. If established it can work itself through different steps to the extent that the conditions allow. If successful, this work will initiate a constructive spiral, which shows both politicians and the population at large, the advantages of a reconciliation process: more security, increased trust, and new possibilities for social and economic initiatives.

This way of thinking implies that a nation-wide and firmly established peace agreement, on its way to completion, is not a necessary condition for at least a partial political reconciliation process. However, it requires a degree of fundamental change on the public level—for instance geographically (regions, cities, actors) and/or politically (cease-fire, demobilization, and the like).

Reconciliation processes in the midst of ongoing violence can take place in certain regions, with certain actors, and on certain dimensions, as a way to demonstrate what this can mean for a nation as a whole. In Colombia there have been examples of regional commissions working on issues of justice and truth, even if the conflict was not settled on the national level between the major guerilla groups and the government. If there is a national commission this gives room for regional commissions. The goal of such partial processes would of course be, to make it deeper in terms of methods and content, and wider in terms of geography. As long as the reconciliation process is not reversed by actors deviating from its fundamental nature, this can be defended both politically and morally.

RECONCILIATION AND FORGIVENESS

By nature, reconciliation—whether political or not—is not a totally individual process, it is social. Anyone involved in reconciliation needs to know that "this is now going on," there is no such thing as unilateral reconciliation. There has to be at least two individuals that can reconcile with each other. In this sense, reconciliation is a *relational* concept.

Reconciliation is providing a tool for building relationships. It is, to use sociological language, a *structural* concept, which for that particular reason can serve in a political context, and not only in a private or individual setting. It is this structural, relation-building capacity of "reconciliation" which makes the concept relevant and useful in a political discourse and practice. This is the basis for the theoretical meaning of "political reconciliation."

Let's consider "forgiveness" in the same way. It is in some respects very different. Forgiveness can be a one-sided act that can be expressed without any reciprocal action from the intended recipient's side. Actually it has the same status as a gift in this respect. A person can be forgiven without knowing about it. It is a unilateral act, from one person to another. Of course, there can be—and there are—so many cases of mutual forgiveness—and they are all fine and may be very good also from a political point of view—but the concept as such does not require this mutuality to happen, in order for it to be a meaningful activity.

As a consequence of this argument, forgiveness, when used in a *political* vocabulary, is anchored in the individual person's perception of what is possible. If forgiveness, for one reason or another is not possible, the concept doesn't work. Instead it becomes problematic and can at worst function as an imposition upon individuals for the sake of something larger, maybe. "Are you ready to forgive?" is then a question, if posed as a public exhortation, that goes against the nature of the whole process, as a voluntary and individual development on the personal level.

So for our continued analysis of "political reconciliation" we will stick to the principle that the concept is based on a relational dimension of communication, between individuals or groups.

POLITICAL RECONCILIATION AND A LANGUAGE OF CONFLICT RESOLUTION

The frequent use of "reconciliation" in various forms of political rhetoric, not the least in connection to major peace processes, such as in Colombia or Burma/Myanmar who both were reaching important stages in 2016, faces the risk of equalizing "conflict resolution" with "political reconciliation."

Interests, motives, and commitments, often in combination with strategy, tactics, and various types of power, are all concepts that are familiar for a conflict analyst. They refer basically to characteristics of individual actors. However, a conflict is by definition a form of interaction between at least two parties, and for that reason, conflict analysis needs as well to include concepts that recognize that mutuality and relationship is an inevitable part of a conflict and conflict resolution process.

RECONCILIATION AS POLITICS

When new concepts are introduced, the first question should of course be: what does this new concept say which is not covered by other concepts? What is the difference between conflict resolution, conflict management, peaceful co-existence, and similar concepts? The answer can be illustrated by reference to a classical figure in early peace research, the conflict triangle.[16] It says, briefly, that three components are necessary for a social conflict to be at hand: attitudes, behavior and an incompatibility—all with at least two actors. Thus the classical triangle consists of the following components:

Figure 2. A conflict triangle

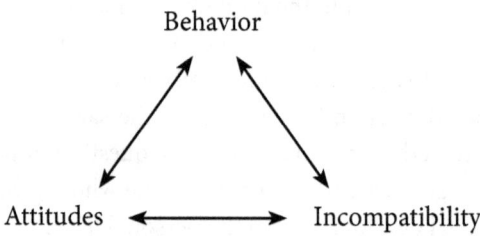

Conflict *behavior* is the "visible outside" of a conflict: the killing, destruction, and all other forms of depriving the enemy of resources. The *incompatibility* is the issue(s) at stake—answering the question: what are the parties fighting for? Sometimes they agree on what they are fighting for, sometimes not. But they are nevertheless fighting. The *attitudes* are, as the concept indicates, all those views, opinions, and predispositions that parties have when thinking about the other side.

It is possible to settle an incompatibility also among the hardest rivals or enemies without reconciling. If they have a common interest in settling the issue, they can do it without changing attitudes about the other side. Now, reconciliation belongs to the attitudinal side of the triangle. Political reconciliation is therefore not about solving political conflicts, it is about *dealing with their consequences*—before or after they are resolved or settled.

Conflict resolution, if we continue going through the concepts, belongs either to the behavioral or to the incompatibility side. This is so because a conflict settlement can be either a type of conflict management (to handle the behavior of parties so that they act non-violently), or of conflict

---

16. The conflict triangle was developed as a concept by Galtung, "Conflict."

resolution (to resolve the matter once and for all by eliminating the incompatibility). Political reconciliation, again, deals with the consequences of conflict and war, mostly the long-term consequences, in the memories and minds of people.

While the three triangular concepts indicate basic dimensions of social conflict, it is a good illustration to identify their peace-time counterparts, so to speak: how can the triangle be developed into a triangle of peace components? Such a process deserves of course another study, but the following concepts may help us en route in that work. The triangle then looks as follows:

Figure 3. A peace triangle

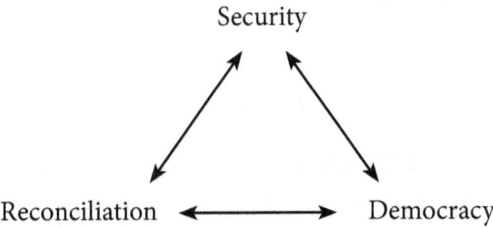

If the *reconciliation* concept deals with attitudes in the most profound way we can arrange on a political level, *democracy* is the way by which a society peacefully can deal with its incompatibilities. Finally, *security*, both in the sense of physical security in social life, as well as a sustainable and thus secure environment, belongs to the last corner of the triangle. This illustrates, and explains, the complementarity of reconciliation in a conflict resolution process, and more importantly, the usefulness of distinguishing between conflict resolution and political reconciliation.

THE RELATIONAL COMPONENT

We have noted that political reconciliation is about the attitudes between individuals and groups. Attitudes are deeply rooted in personalities and group mentalities and they have both a cognitive component and an emotional. A legal process, on the other hand, is designed so as to keep attitudes under control: heads should be held cool also in the most grim and repugnant circumstances. Also, court proceedings do not normally involve any form of message or interaction between victim and perpetrator. In court proceedings the two sides try to convince the court, not each other.

In a reconciliation process the situation is different. Relations are critical and a major purpose of reconciliation is to influence relations. But what is a reasonable way of thinking in terms of attitudes? Should all the enemies suddenly be friends?

First, becoming friends is (of course) not the purpose of political reconciliation, it would be naïve and simplistic. Second, it is not a given, that relations should be restored to "what they were" before conflict. All in all, those historic relations were somehow linked to a situation that went out of hand. So, again, what is then an "appropriate" level and nature of "post—political reconciliation" relations?

Three types of relations can be identified in order to maintain an agreed political settlement. Let's go through them one by one.

Former Enemies Need to Uphold Functional Relations

If actors from the battlefield have negotiated and agreed on, for instance, a comprehensive peace agreement there is a moral duty upon them to maintain their level of communication over the agreement and its repercussions. This is so, not only because the agreement is from their hand, but because of the power to change society that comes from the agreement's clauses. Power produces responsibility, a responsibility to protect the agreement and this includes as well a responsibility to communicate functionally over the future of the agreement. Parties, that is, top-level actors, who also are politically reconciled are more likely to be able to uphold such a relationship than other actors.

Civil Society and Political Leaders Need to Be Peace-Supportive

Part of educating a society about the utility and advantages of a peaceful and, as much as possible, democratic political system is the role model function which leaders of ideological, religious, and interest groups play. This includes respect for a negotiated compromise, and not a continued "fight" to the extent that the whole agreement is jeopardized.

State Administrators Need to Be Non-Discriminating

Nothing is as easy as to continue discriminatory practices in a work and duty that has all the incentives for bribery, discrimination, and bullying. For state employees, who represent the first face, the first level of contacts with the state, for the individual citizen, a profoundly new relation to citizens is an often overlooked aspect of peace-building.

What this produces is a number of reconciliation-building initiatives related to peace processes. Pre-agreement reconciliation as well as post-agreement long-term processes of truth and reparation are all to be commended. However, certain aspects are critical at the turning point, at the transition from conflict and war to stability and an emerging peace.

RECONCILIATION AS A GENDER DIMENSION

It fits into a traditional and a male-dominated cultural view—often called patriarchal—to say that reconciliation, whether in politics or social life in general, is not a serious concept in politics, but an approach to conflict and conflict resolution that signals allegedly feminine features: weakness, readiness to compromise, and a general uneasiness of conflict. "Reconciliation," one can note, is not the only concept that has been, and still is, exposed to such delusive generalizations—the first being maybe "peace" itself.

Political reconciliation has to deal with at least three major areas where women, and often children, are exposed to systematic violence or discrimination: as targets or soldiers in armed conflict, as overridden potential actors in peace processes, and as overlooked beneficiaries in reparation programs.

Gender-based violence belongs to those features of armed conflict that had not been described and taken into account unless there had been a combination of theoretical tools for their analytical identification and an active political effort for their introduction. Traditional military history writers either dismissed or neglected this reality for long. As members of civil society, women and children are the most exposed groups to direct (or indirect) violence and other causes of suffering, based on ongoing violence and conflict. The effect of this is, that those that should play the most significant roles in rebuilding a society are at the same time targeted the most, among civilians.

To many readers, mere facts and figures about systematic rape, exploitation and sexual attacks are shocking, and graphic stories about real such events are beyond what many can take in. Such descriptions are however based on wide-spread cultural and strategic practices in many countries—in particular in societies pendulating between day-time "stability" and night-time war fighting—but also countries where even the most rudimentary security is lost due to economic interests, which set up their own security forces, and a total fragmentation of public security.

While exposed to violence, the position of women in a society is at the same time a strategic one, from a peace and reconciliation perspective. This is so for reasons that go counter to the patriarchal view sketched above. Women know suffering at the heart of society, where the weakest members of the society live, and not seldom from their own experience. Women as a group knows the life-sustaining conditions of societies—just exactly the competence that is needed for rebuilding a community after any catastrophe.

UN Security Council Resolution 1325 has helped to remind actors about the role women can take, as actors in peace processes. It is a landmark resolution for peace processes globally. It was passed in 2000 and has since then paved the way for further UN resolutions focusing on particular areas, for instance recognizing sexual violence as a tactic, ending impunity for perpetrators, and reproductive health services to affected women.[17]

Truth as a Gender Tool

It is easy to go on with examples of very unsatisfactory conditions in peace processes, from a gender perspective: peace agreements are marginally signed by women, peace mediators are rarely seen in high-level mediation processes, etcetera. A general impression from the literature is that reconciliation processes are less analyzed from a gender perspective than peace processes in general.

Truth Commissions—with or without a reconciliation component—suffer from male domination in their composition as most other institutionalised forums in the North and South likewise. The battle for the moment is not only to create a more balanced gender relation, but also to bring in perspectives of the weakest gender of a situation into the process—whether

---

17. UN Security Council resolutions 1820, 1960, and 2122, respectively, deal with these measures.

women or men exposed to sexual violence, children or elderly suffering from malnutrition etc. For this to happen, women's organizations are crucial in peace processes in general and reconciliation processes specifically.

What many authors stress, is the role of truth for establishing gender justice. The single most important tool for a gender sensitive approach to political reconciliation is a truth process—whether factual, written, and testimonial or told, shared, and performed. The more free, the better.

Since patriarchy benefits from legal proceedings, due to inbuilt structural injustices reflected in such processes, truth is a critical concept and practice in order to establish gender justice and therefore a basis for reconciliation.

With a focus on truth, the oppression of rulers, the sexual exploitation of soldiers, the domestic violence of returning soldiers, the systematic use of rape and sexual violence as strategic warfare—all become at least told and therefore exposed to light. This is the first basis for further action and cannot be stressed enough. From an increasing knowledge about this and similar violations, a basis for action can be built, also for reconciliation. Without knowledge about "what to reconcile about" it is less likely to happen, to say the least.

This link between truth and a gender analysis of traditionally male areas of society is a revealing example of the need for multiple theoretical perspectives in social science and politics. The combination of roles and a power, a typical gender analysis combination, therefore puts a demand on the nature of any reconciliation process, if it should not only be sensitive, but structurally indifferent, to gender dimensions.

CHANGING MIND?

Imagine a perpetrator and his/her attitude to the victims and to the society before an awaiting legal process. From this person we do not, and cannot, legally demand a change of mind in the direction of contrition, in order for him/her to pass the process, including its judgment. (A change of mind can affect the decision of the court, but the point here is the opposite: the court cannot enforce contrition.) There may be bold ambitions of the prison system to change and develop a person under its protection. Nevertheless, he/she will not have to change mind in order to get freedom at a certain date. Once again, "good behavior," etc. can in some systems shorten the time, but that's not the point here.

RECONCILIATION AS POLITICS

It is hard to imagine as meaningful a process of reconciliation where there is no change of attitude whatsoever. At the same time, this is something that cannot be forced upon anyone. Thus, a process of reconciliation, and a commission that organizes such a process, needs to seek out the extent to which extent a change of mind this is at all possible to achieve and, in a particular case, present.

A consequence of this view is that, theoretically speaking, if all atrocities and violations etc. that have taken place during a given conflict are dealt with within an established, regular legal/court system, that would not be an example of a reconciliation process.

Reconciliation is in this sense "wider" than a legal process, it concerns a reality that a court may not be able to reach—at least not legally—which deals with the web of responsibilities, hidden goals, and deceptions that become part of daily life in protracted armed conflict situations, even if they are very human, so necessary for survival and decent management of day-to-day life. Again, reconciliation points to the change of attitudes among those involved.

There is also an attitudinal dimension in "political reconciliation," that individuals and others would like to send when they reconcile. The fundamental message is, that an individual, a group, or even a country is prepared to reconsider, on the basis of new arguments or a reassessment of the situation, legitimate claims (moral, legal, material) against the other person/side, for the sake of re-establishing relations based on the perpetrator's acknowledgement of the victim's suffering and a responsibility in this connection. The various components mentioned above, making up a "reconciliation process"—such as acknowledgement, contrition, truth telling, reparation, and justice—are all instruments for this.

Reconciliation processes, with their different mechanisms, deal with a situation that a society's regular institutions are not built for, and therefore are not able to deal with effectively, neither legally nor socially or ethically. This is a transitional state of affairs, and a truth and reconciliation commission should therefore as soon as possible be replaced by permanent institutional arrangements for dealing with history, memories and interpretations of the past.

THE UNILATERAL APOLOGY

Is a unilateral apology an example of political reconciliation? It may seem like a reconciliatory act, to ask for forgiveness, but when we reflect over its nature, the conclusion has to be, that it is in fact far from.

When Chief Executive Officers apologize for products that fail to meet promised standards, or when politicians are found with a finger in the cookie jar, they sometimes unilaterally and unconditionally apologize—they make a poodle. Public relations advisors have at some point told them that this is the right thing to do, if there shall ever be a way out in the clean air again. Whatever their personal view, the public will read the situation in its own way, and finally be the judge. It is a relatively recent phenomenon, that it is at all politically possible to survive after having publically been identified as lacking moral capacity to be a leader. Some analysts would refer to the personalization of politics as a reason, others to a lack of respect for leaders. One can hypothesize and say, that authoritarian leaders do not benefit from apologizing, and democratic leaders (including company leaders with a similar profile) show their human, democratic face by doing so, and may therefore survive with this act within a democracy.

In this chapter we are however concerned with the politically much more serious—but in principle similarly designed—approach to moral challenges in political situations, and that is the demand for an apology directed towards governments, individual leaders, or major international organizations. These demands range from community mistreatment of children in public homes, nation-building atrocities and discrimination against for instance indigenous populations, and to genocide victims and historically discriminated peoples.

So far, we have been concerned with political reconciliation as an act of mutual responsiveness to morally challenging demands, based on a certain degree of relation-building. But when Germany's president at the time, apologizes for the bombing of Coventry Cathedral fifty years later, or when the Japanese prime minister apologizes for comfort women at the disposal of the Japanese army, or when the prime ministers of Australia and of Canada in 2008 apologize (in separate national manifestations) for their country's treatment of their respective indigenous populations—when these things happen, relation-building is not a pre-condition, but rather a possible consequence.

The unilateral apology is an *invitation* to relation-building, and therefore a demanding act, since it both exposes both the individual, or a government, expressing an apology to an open reaction situation, and, at the same time, invites and puts a demand on those that are victimized to come forward and in some way respond.

In campaigns or demands on a broader scale, for the rectification of historical injustices, there is an interesting difference between cases where what is to be rectified are events or acts which *also when they were committed*, were considered wrong and evil, and therefore were committed in the dark—as compared to acts or social systems that once were *openly practiced* but where our society today condemns this historic practice.

The former case is easier for a political community to deal with, since it is basically an empirical question to what extent and on what scale certain atrocities were carried out. A normative discussion is however not necessary to develop, since the views on what happened are unchanged from those days till today.

How unilateral apologies are received, followed-up and developed further is still an area lacking systematic research, but it is an interesting addition to the menu of possible political acts. Of course, it has its characteristics and requires a presentation on par with the dignity of its content. Again, in the context of political reconciliation it is rather an invitation to reconcile, than a reconciliatory act in itself. It is an attempt at relation-building, asking for forgiveness sometimes, but not necessarily so. It does polish relations, but to the extent it reconciles, remains to be seen and is dependent on the practices that follow after the unilateral apologizing act.

DEFINING POLITICAL RECONCILIATION

As a broad definition of what is political reconciliation, given what we have discussed so far, would be to say that political reconciliation is a process where harm caused by political violence is repaired in such a way that a basic level of trust again is established. "Harm," then, is a consequence both of injustices in a legal sense as well as of violations of human dignity that may not be covered by law. "Repaired" refers to a variety of acts and processes that various mechanisms in a process can provide, each of them hopefully tailored to a specific context, such as acknowledgement, symbolic acts, truth telling, material reparation/compensation, legal justice, and common mourning. In some cultures, the fulfillment of local and/or traditional mechanisms are as important as any other process; in other cultures, the legal dimension appears to be the primary, setting others aside, while in yet other cultures, the group-oriented and religious dimension takes precedence over other.

Hopefully, and critical for the whole process, is that human dignity is restored through these different mechanisms. This is easily said, but on the basis of dignity comes the possibility for victims to turn from being an "object"—for other's acts—to becoming a "subject," taking initiatives based on one's own resources.

"Trust" is here a key word. It refers to what can be described as "social trust" meaning the fundamental type of relationship in a society that, without it, there would be no valid promises, no fundamental security in the street, etc. ("Trust" in this sense lies between "confidence," which includes sharing of information, and "acceptance" which is what is demanded from everyone towards another person, irrespective of their personal differences.)

An interesting aspect in this is the component of *over-looking* old events and current claims that on good grounds can be made on the basis of these events. These claims can be moral or legal, sometimes dealing with economic or material things (land, live-stock, destroyed economic production units, etc.). However, "for the sake of something better," there can be very different reasons and motivations behind. Anyway a new path of relations is chosen: a harbor, a school etc. is rebuilt through common effort since everybody needs it and benefits from it. "Over-looking" does not at all have to mean "forget," or "pardon/forgive," but it brings, through making a claim relative to other claims, a fresh air into the dialogue of a community—temporarily or lasting. Such a change is something that no one can ask for from outside, but it nevertheless can emerge from within, given the situation that exists.

From this we can see, that political reconciliation is a somewhat different thing than reconciliation in general. First, "political" reconciliation is a process dealing with injustice due to *political conflict*. Second, since it takes place on the political level, it has to be cognizant and respectful of its limitations when it comes to integrity and *respect for the individual dimension* in reconciliation processes, as we have noted in relation to the concept of forgiveness, and "over-looking" above.

A political reconciliation process has finally a *societal dimension* to it, which is different from inter-personal reconciliation. An issue on the political level is not only a matter between the victim and a perpetrator personally. If they have reconciled then it is a matter for the society as a

RECONCILIATION AS POLITICS

whole—everyone has the right to know, that political reconciliation has taken place.

The encouraging and positive development that can come out from reconciliation becomes then known to everybody whether directly or indirectly affected. This final feature is a clear difference from private/individual forms of reconciliation. In the latter, no one can claim the right to know what two parties do to their relationship, in principle.

After this discussion, a more complete descriptive definition can be formulated, saying that political reconciliation is *a social process where harm, resulting from political violence, is repaired in such a way that basic trust is established between victims, perpetrators, and the society at large.*

What is of interest is of course what factors there are, that will create such a social process. To identify these will be our main task in pages to come.

2

Whose Truth and Which Reconciliation?

TRUTH AND JUSTICE

Besides the legal system that every state has, there are at least two other types of legal systems that also claim relevance in certain situations. These are on the one hand legal systems of indigenous peoples, and on the other hand the international legal system, whether integrated in the state-based legislation or not.

When it comes to indigenous peoples, a lot of work is done by governments as well as by (representatives of) indigenous peoples to define and relate official and indigenous systems to each other.[1] In other cases, such as East Timor/Timor Leste,[2] neither the colonial nor the occupying power entered so deep into the Timorese society so as to eradicate or even change much of the traditional systems of law and social order. The United Nations, on its part, established in Timor Leste a formal justice system during the United Nations Transitional Administration in East Timor (UNTAET) transitional period, without relating effectively to existing legal practices, however with one important exception—the traditional community reconciliation practice, *Badame*.

---

1. For an example, see Colmenares Olívar, *Los Derechos*.
2. "East Timor" will be used with reference to the period up to independence in 2002. Thereafter the official name of the new state, "Timor Leste," is used in this text, as a rule.

RECONCILIATION AS POLITICS

The establishment in 2001 of the Commission for Reception, Truth and Reconciliation[3] in East Timor, included in the UNTAET legislation for the Commission a reference to a traditional conflict resolution mechanism in the East Timorese society, practiced since centuries, a system of community based reconciliation methods, often called "Badame," meaning "the road to peace" in Tetum, the country's lingua franca. The Badame process was, and is, well established from village level and beyond. It is also today practiced in the Timor Leste capital Dili, whenever certain matters should be sorted out in particular within family law, and minor criminal offences. The UN agreed to include a role for the Badame process within the larger scheme of legislation surrounding the work of the Commission. It dealt with less serious crimes, i.e., with non-lethal consequences or without constituting crimes against humanity; these minor offences were allowed to be passed on to the local level. Serious crimes that were revealed in the work of the Commission should however be brought to the attention of the Serious Crimes Unit, a special court procedure set up by the UN in the capital Dili to deal with these crimes.

The state's legal system is simply not accepted in all situations, and to this author a person in Timor Leste stated, that the sentences meted out by the international UN court may be correct from an international point of view, but not necessarily from a national Timorese point of view. "Those sentences are more for the comfort of your conscience, than of ours."

Thus, a person who passes through the regular court system, for instance someone who is released after a fulfilled term of sentence, is on the local level not necessarily regarded as a "free" person. He/she may still have to go through the local reconciliation process, and pay the price that is connected to that, in order to be accepted again, by the local community.

We will return to this discussion in later chapters. What we can note already here is, that this fact, of three normative systems with claims to be relevant in the same situations, is in itself an unsatisfactory situation from any point of view.

The need for coordination does not only concern local, traditional forms of justice. Also between the national and international levels of justice is a need for clarification and maybe adjustment. We should however note here, that a main principle for the work by the ICC, besides that it cannot act retroactively on events before its inception, is that it should take

---

3. In Portuguese, an official language in Timor Leste, the Commission is called Comissão de Acolhimento, Verdade e Reconciliação, CAVR.

action only when the national legal system is not dealing at all, or inappropriately, with a particular case.

In a Colombian debate over a legislation in June 2005 (called the Law on Peace and Justice and connected to demobilization of the para-military groups at the time) many argued for the need of tuning the law to international standards, since it was constructed as generous enough for the groups to consider a return to civil life, in spite of being fully armed and not defeated militarily. It remains to be seen where the borderline goes. Obviously, impunity is a clear line that many want to draw: there shall always be a cost for those that have committed serious violations and human rights abuses.

In the case of the peace process of Sierra Leone, impunity given to some leaders as part of a national peace agreement was in practice over-ruled by the international court set up in the country to deal with crimes against humanity and against International Humanitarian Law. This is however a different situation than the Colombian. In the case of Sierra Leone, there was no national legal process included in the agreement whatsoever—with or without impunity. In Colombia the regular court system was about to proceed with the cases if and when all conditions were set.

In order for a peace process, including its legal parts, to be legitimate in the eyes of the local population and the parties themselves, it is necessary that it is carried out inside the country, by its own courts if at all possible, and on the basis of national legislation. That would be the most preferred situation. Again, the Sierra Leone case is unfortunately an example of a legal process out of touch with the national political and legal situation. The International War Crimes Tribunal in Cambodia, dealing with a group of Khmer Rouge leaders, has had the same problem of isolation on the national level. Also in Timor Leste, the sentences from the Serious Crimes Unit have in some instances been sharply criticized as out of proportion, given the low ranks of those convicted. This had the effect of alienating the Court and its role as a confidence-building instrument for the population and the nation as a whole.

It is important that if a national legal system, its police, courts and prisons, should contribute to building a stable and peaceful environment for the society, it has to actively seek support and legitimacy from the nation it serves. Thus, it has to relate to the conditions prevailing in that society also in the post-war situation that there is. What are the resources, competencies available for carrying out justice? With what degree of security and resources can witnesses be brought in, offenders kept in detention, prisons be managed?

Some of these questions are closely related to the important distinction between negotiated and imposed agreements. Obviously, in negotiated agreements situations, there is much less leeway for actions against perpetrators, than in imposed. Also, the general capacity of a state is a major aspect to be considered: building up a national legal system, its buildings, its procedures and its staff, takes of course years.

TRUTH-TELLING

One of the most well-known truth and reconciliation commissions was the one in South Africa in the 1990s. Truth-telling was a most significant part of its work. Many believed at the time, that the mere telling of the truth would also work reconciliatory, that it would help healing people on the individual level. Analyzes after some time show that this may have been too high expectations.

The purpose with the truth component, as explained by truth commissions, is not to heal in the first place, but to recognize, to acknowledge and bring into light hidden parts of an individual's and a society's past. Another important aspect is, that to give information to a truth commission should not be mixed up with giving a testimony for a court. Testifying to a court means answering to the court's questions and needs, but to tell one's own story in a statement to a truth commission is something totally decided in content by the witness. One's own truth is what is conveyed, to somebody that is interested (read: a truth commission). This statement will then, supposedly, be an important part of a country's, a community's common history. As a secondary consequence of this, an individual may very well feel acknowledged, which is part of a healing process, even if it has its limits. To take statements is a very different activity from trauma healing, both in terms of practice and the necessary competence—it is important to keep expectations on an appropriate level.

At this point it should be noted, that also perpetrators need to get their stories told—for their own sake and for the society as a whole. When it comes to this perspective, the perpetrators are heard in courts much more than anywhere else.

An interesting and important second phase of truth telling is the history-making part of it. If the stories—each person's story about his/her truth—were not told, there would be a risk in the future, that the history of what has happened would be re-written in the interest of some groups, and at the expense of others. Truth commissions normally have as their task to summarize and draw conclusions in different ways. The statements as such speak for themselves, but sometimes more historical conclusions are drawn, with recommendations for how a society in the future can avoid a development of the same kind, again.[4]

If there were no documents at hand, no evidence presented and if people never had been given the possibility to freely tell their story, a country would be more fragile and exposed to historical mistakes in the future. This was an explicit South African philosophy in the 1990s and there is a lot to it.

WHICH RECONCILIATION?

We have noted that the concept of reconciliation can be used to describe both the goal of a process, and the process itself. What is important to observe, is that in this process each step requires a relation between at least two individuals. This makes "reconciliation" fundamentally different from, for instance, "forgiveness." You can forgive even without mentioning it to the forgiven person—if the person is alive—and a person can ask for forgiveness but being denied this. In addition, to forgive does not, as a concept, require a change of mind or any compensation on part of the individual that is forgiven—even if this may very well happen many times. But this lack of requirement on the "targeted" person is the strength and unique quality of "forgiveness"—forgiveness is totally in the hands of the one who forgives and without any expectation of the one that is forgiven. The possibility of "forgiveness" to be a unilateral instrument for offering something for free, is its strength. To widen the use, or meaning of "forgiveness," means in practice a blurring of the concept. By employing it on the group level, and in addition within the political sphere, is therefore not to show respect for the concept's specific character. Anyway, people do forgive each other and that is great—it is not an uncommon part of life within families and among friends, albeit a difficult one.

    4. In Timor Leste, where the report from the Commission for Reception, Truth and Reconciliation was handed over to the president on October 30, 2005, more than 400 statement-takers traveled around the country and collected thousands of stories. An early example of this way of working was the Guatemalan Commission for Historical Clarification in 1994. This commission was however severely constrained by the level of information it was able to publish, due to the political situation in the country at the time.

RECONCILIATION AS POLITICS

These characteristics of "forgiveness" render, as already noticed, the concept very inappropriate, not to say useless, in a political context. Politics is by nature relation-building, it is collective work among collectives. Individual processes of relation-building are part of politics but need to be open—the political sphere shall give space for such processes, in particular when social and individual healing is necessary, but the process of forgiveness can and should never be set to follow a pace or a program according to political interests. "Reconciliation"—on the other hand—can address a bilateral situation in a way that "forgiveness" cannot.

Let's consider the specific nature of "reconciliation." As we have seen, to "reconcile" is not possible to do unilaterally—it is always built on a relation. Even if we accept that a relation is the basis for reconciliation, it is not obvious that it can take place. It requires a change of mind in some way, and so by at least one individual (or group) in this relationship. Because of this, "reconciliation" is a concept with a political potentiality. It has the internal structure to contribute to a conceptual political toolbox by addressing collective relations.

THE SAME REALITY BUT DIFFERENT TRUTHS?

Societies are normally not divided to the level of polarization that is common in internal armed conflicts, even in conflicts based on identity lines. There are sometimes friendships, marriages, neighborhood relations, and common economic interests that cross over divisions that leaders want to draw. Many in the Balkan states in Europe wonder today how it could happen that their seemingly mixed and stable societies in a short time, became so divided that neighbors or colleagues could carry out the most horrendous acts against each other. There were also many who stood against such tendencies, it should be noted. There was a lot of assistance on the personal level crossing ethnic group lines. Many conflict situations show examples of this.

The conclusion we can make is, that when all things are considered, the situation is not white and black neither in terms of loyalty nor in terms of responsibility. In order to adjust and correct the dominating, often propagandistic picture of a conflict, stories about single events, heroic initiatives as well as everyday minor support, among a struggling people—in the midst of war—need to be told and documented. The leader's and professional history writer's view about what happened is not and should not for the future be the only source of reference.

It is a commonly held view, that establishing the "truth" (whatever this means) is a necessary condition for "reconciliation." "Truth" is then, according to this view, a *sine qua non* for reconciliation. There is reason to accept that. Turning to the legal system we find that it establishes "a truth" in relation to the requirements of the law, the morally based processes of reconciliation are free to take another view. Obviously, our view of what is "truth" impacts our view of what is an adequate form for reconciliation.

APPLYING A LIBERAL AND A COMMUNITARIAN PERSPECTIVE

How can we look upon different ways to describe the truth? Broadly speaking, it is possible to make a distinction between a "liberal" and a "communitarian" view of "truth."

If we—with full respect for the variations a liberal position may contain—propose a view of "liberal truth" as based on empirical facts, rationality, objectivity, and logical reasoning, this is very different in substance from what can be described as a "communitarian truth." From a communitarian point of view, shared knowledge and experiences, and values, and practices that are all shared in a community, are key to what is considered as the truth, both about an individual as well as a social and even existential environment. A communitarian truth, then, may contain internal contradictions because it does not necessarily reflect a certain view on what is a contradiction, and what is not. Life is full of contradictions, and so could be the case also with what is called "truth." While this is a problem from a liberal point of view it is not necessarily so, from a communitarian point of view.

It seems, that in peace processes, the legal dimension represents—for instance in international courts and panels—a liberal view, while the reconciliation process, on a group and individual level, represents a more communitarian perspective. It may also seem, as a consequence of this, that these perspectives could complement each other, and that we should basically be comforted by the multi-faceted approach that peace processes can take. People are different, have different needs, and a peace process needs to be adapted to this variation. There is some value in such a position. I would however argue here, that for a *society* that tries to heal itself from the scars of internal conflict, a communitarian truth is more likely to serve such a purpose in the long run, since the relational component in the communitarian position is explicit and substantial. Or put differently: since a rational, objective, and logical truth is "self-sufficient" (from its self-evident foundations) and thus is only vaguely a relation-building form of truth, it is not a *sufficient* truth for restoring social trust. It is therefore a necessary but not sufficient component of a process towards "reconciliation."

It is only natural at this point to put the question of what are the implications for reconciliation efforts, given the differences between the two perspectives. These differences can be hinted at, through the summary made in Table 3.

Table 3. Possible implications of Liberal and Communitarian perspectives on the truth concept

	Dimension of truth	Example of component
Liberal perspective on truth	Rational	Law decides what is relevant information
	Empirical	Compensations as "reparation"
	Logical	Same deed = same penitence
Communitarian perspective on truth	Shared	All relevant information is a contribution
	Experienced	Reparation as the victim's needs satisfaction
	Wholeness	Mutual acknowledgement is part of understanding

The liberal view will result in an understanding of the concept of political reconciliation as a fact-based process where the individual is compensated—materially and/or psychologically—for harm caused by politically motivated acts. Through this process, human dignity is restored. Compensation is basically individual, but can be group oriented if the group can be defined in a satisfactory way.

A communitarian view would argue that restoring human dignity is a community-based process, where reconciliation is a tool for the wider conception of identity and dignity, concepts related to each other. Reconciliation, then, is embedded in a shared understanding of both facts and feelings, where the interpretation is not only shared but also developed in common. Since hurting the individual is hurting a community in this perspective, also reconciliation in its compensation parts has a community component.

IS POLITICAL RECONCILIATION CONFLICT RESOLUTION?

It is important to realize, that reconciliation is different from conflict resolution and conflict management. While conflict resolution and conflict management are concepts that refer to the *treatment of issues*, that is the substantial matters that motivated the conflict in the first place, these issues can be settled without reconciliation. In the same way, the more superficial treatment of a conflict—which is to stop *conflict behavior*, that is to stop the killing and destruction—is for obvious reasons not at all similar to reconciliation. So both these corners in the conflict triangle, presented in the first chapter, are independent from each other, in terms of the settlement of a conflict.

What remains now of the content of "conflict," since we have already dealt with the behavior and the issues? It is the *attitudes* of the parties. Attitudes, as we know them, have both a cognitive and an emotional component. It is this attitudinal dimension of the conflict as a social phenomenon, which is directly affected by a reconciliation process. Reconciliation, then, means a change of attitudes of the parties, a process that involves both mind and feelings.

As we have seen, reconciliation is, and should be, separated from conflict resolution, and we can have one without the other. This is true also for the connection between reconciliation and conflict behavior—it is meaningless to reconcile if the destruction and the killing continues, to do so would be to blindfold oneself before reality.

On the basis of what we have observed so far, a number of characteristics have emerged from our reflection on the concept of reconciliation in a political context. We are now ready to give a first part of an answer to the question of what could be the contribution of concept of reconciliation.

FIVE FEATURES OF POLITICAL RECONCILIATION

It is possible to identify five distinguishing features of the concept of reconciliation in a political context. Let us consider each of them from the view of a society that has been fragmented in its social web by political violence and conflict.

The first feature is the recognition of the importance of the *meeting with "the other."* The meeting, as a social act, stand as an event that opposes the preference of the individualistic, the singular, and the uniform, which all are dimensions that go against community building.

The second feature is the recognition that there is a *moral dimension* in this meeting, i.e., that implies a recognition that we are moral subjects and objects, this is part of our role as interacting human beings.

The third feature is the recognition of the respective parties that they need the other party in order to understand *their own history* and experience. This has implications for both our cognitive and emotive person. Actually this is a critical moment in the reconciliation process.

The fourth feature is that it includes the recognition of the need to make history a *never repeated* history. Those involved in reconciliation, are likely to be concerned with the non-repetition of their own experience, since it will hurt both sides.

The fifth feature of the concept of political reconciliation is that *it is public*. It is never private, secret, or hidden if it is a genuine political act. This is so because of the very nature of politics, of political acts and of political life in general—it concerns the network of relations that we create by free will, for our common good and the welfare of everyone. So if the violence was political, then the healing should be political and public.

RECONCILIATION AS A THEORETICAL CONCEPT

If we would like to define "reconciliation" in a way that makes the concept possible to use in theoretical statements, in a theory about society for instance, it should be defined so as to be adequate for this task, both descriptively and theoretically. In addition, we deal in this case with a concept that covers acts which from the beginning are morally difficult to justify, so there is a normative dimension as well to be taken care of.

If we begin with the normative aspect, and apply it to the concept of "reconciliation" we will find, first, that the acts for which "reconciliation" are relevant should be those that are normatively unacceptable (or in stronger words: unjustifiable). Only those acts will be part of a reconciliation process.

Second, "reconciliation" needs to be defined in a way that is largely in line with a common understanding about what it is that takes place among people that reconcile, and finally and thirdly: the concept should be defined in a way that makes it possible to use in a theoretical statement, such as: "if reconciliation, then durable peace." A theoretical statement is in this context seen as a concept which can be tested on empirical grounds.

Now, if we employ such criteria on the contribution of the concept of reconciliation to the political language—which elements do we find? Are there new elements to be found?

I think so and we will work on it further in this text. We need a concept in the political vocabulary that recognizes the social and human dimensions of political processes. Peace processes are better equipped, conceptually speaking, in their initial stages than in their final. Stalemate, cease-fire, "talks-about-talks," facilitation, mediation, and negotiation—they are all concepts for the early or middle phases of a peace process. "Reconciliation" has the potential—if we clarify what we mean with the concept—to be a useful concept for guiding understanding of the final phases of a peace process, something that we need for both theoretical, political, and—not the least—human reasons.

3

Five Ways of Dealing with the Past

In previous chapters we have noted that concepts like "justice," "truth," "reconciliation," and "democracy," together with more technical concepts such as "cease-fire" and "elections," are well entrenched agenda issues in peace processes after civil wars, or after periods of dictatorship. We noted also that this development gained momentum from some early and challenging cases in Latin America in the past century, but also from cases in Africa with the fall of the Apartheid regime in South Africa as a prominent case. In this case there was significant international attention paid to its nation-wide truth and reconciliation process. What these cases have in common is, that they represent an alternative to older and more traditional mechanisms of dealing with the past.

THE NEED OF TIME

Each social process, involving individual experiences, requires time and respect for the individual's pace for dealing with the past. This reflects a classical tension between the needs for (quick) political action and social development, on the one hand, and respect for the individual on the other. The important dimension of the dilemma may not be how it can be solved, but how it can be managed. Is it possible to allow for individual, often mental, processes to take their time, while at the same time initiating a national process which creates a fundamental change in group relations? Or is it necessary to wait for a change of mind to "materialize" among broad layers of the population?

One aspect of this is the observation that although a conflict is settled in an agreement, there are most likely remaining issues "out there" to which individuals and groups, also after an agreement on the political level, feel more or less concerned about. Such contextual conditions make all kinds of planning of a reconciliation process preliminary. And it is sometimes difficult to obtain resources that are necessary for dealing with such problems, since they are normally not on the radar for international development assistance.

Nevertheless there are many people looking at political reconciliation as something necessary and something that may be the only available means at hand in a post-conflict situation. Better try once than never, is their view.

THE NEED OF TRUTH

Some would argue that it is better to refrain from initiating such a process, than having a half-measure. Others would say that if one never begins, there will never be a beginning. If the peace agreement is *the* turning point, then it is not natural to go on with "business as usual," since the coming peace period is different, it is based on different premises for social activity compared to what it was before, during conflict. When people and memories are alive the memories can be remembered, told, and documented in a way that could never be done later, that is one of the arguments. It should be seen as a memento for the future, protecting future political systems from forgetting their history.

The introduction of reconciliation in a political context has been a parallel development to the creation of war crime tribunals. These tribunals have had the purpose to deal specifically with war crimes committed in a specific conflict during a specific time period. Such tribunals/panels are not new in the international political history. The post-Second World War Nuremberg Trials are maybe the most well known in the twentieth century. Today, conflicts in Rwanda, Liberia, East Timor, Sierra Leone, and (the breakup of) Yugoslavia, have all been followed by such tribunals. Normally, truth and reconciliation commissions do not have a legal mandate. The South African Truth and Reconciliation Commission could however facilitate and promote amnesty if a perpetrator fully cooperated with the commission and disclosed information. The TRC then represents not a standard but an almost unique model in this respect compared to many such commissions. The most common role for the commissions is to reveal the truth—through statement-taking, open hearings or regular interviews and other forms of documentation—and make it known as widely as possible. In addition, various forms of reconciliation processes, local as well as national, can be used along with systems of material or symbolic compensation or reparation.

It is a widely accepted assumption, both among practitioners and theoreticians of political reconciliation, that the "truth," as far as it can be established, is a necessary if not sufficient component on the road towards a settlement with the past—irrespective of which priority or approach one is taking on other aspects of reconciliation. The question is rather about what "truth" stands for. Is a comprehensive, logical, and matter-of-fact based description of a situation or an event the "truth?" Most people would probably agree that the same event be assessed in different ways depending on the point of reference that different individuals or institutions can have, such as courts, mediators, victims, perpetrators, by-standers. "Truth" is a classic problem in situations of violence and war ("the first victim in war is the truth" as the saying goes), but that is "truth" only in one sense of the word.

For a long-term process, such as the understanding and interpretation of a series of events, "truth" has a deeper meaning, where the relation between intentions and causal chains between events are analyzed. This is even more pronounced in long term, political reconciliation processes. In addition to this, in the end of a truth-seeking activity lies often a question of "meaning." For many involved in political reconciliation it is the existentially relevant truth that is in focus, i.e., a truth that relates to those existential questions that are relevant for that person. Thus, the questions can vary in content and circumstance, but they refer to a level of understanding that is beyond a descriptive account. This is so because conflict, as an armed confrontation with deadly threats and a lot of suffering on all sides, is something that threatens life and central values, often about identity and even faith. It is no wonder that such events in a society raise fundamental questions about life.

If we go on with other truth seeking institutions, a court will connect the information it has been able to obtain, to the legal requirements of the process. Its focus is guided by the legal relevance of facts and other information. This focus may not necessarily be in accordance with what people in general would judge as a morally or contextually relevant information for a given situation or problem. This is not only a matter of whether decisions by a court are in accordance with a common opinion about what the outcome should be of a case, but it has to do with the relevance of the court's proceedings for clarifying a complex event more generally. Often there are too high expectations on legal processes, it is a common view that if we bring an issue to the court it will all be sorted out. This is of course not a natural law.

To establish a comprehensive and as logical overview of an event as possible, is of course of value to all, also to those that criticize a too empirical understanding of "truth." Even if one also would accept that it is in principle impossible to achieve a final such overview. Ideally such a picture should be rational and without contradictions. If there are such type of problems this is most likely due to a methodological problem of the overview, rather than in the assumption of a rational reality that can be fully understood in its manifestations.

So far so good, one may think, but the descriptive aspect of the truth is not the final one, in the case of reconciliation. Although establishing the facts about what has happened and why it happened, it is a classic task of truth and reconciliation commissions, to go beyond this level if the commission shall contribute with something new. At the same time, the full responsibility of making an analysis of the history does not lie with the commission. It is a challenge for individuals as well as groups and politically responsible actors in a society to do their own analysis, and draw their conclusions. This is one of the points in having a truth commission. The commission can give space for reflections, and in this way allow for a society to formulate and interpret its own history. This is a common task, it should not be limited to the capacity of an ever as competent commission.

In this wider work, beyond the descriptive truth, comes the moral truth: what is a morally relevant piece of information (is there a common moral foundation for mankind at all?), and the subsequent and already mentioned existentially relevant truth: Which conditions made me an offender—in spite of starting out life for doing something else? Why did I become a victim, and, is there a meaning in this, or not?

The descriptive, cultural, and existential dimensions of truth become for the individual—whether offender, victim, or both—a story of intertwined elements. Of course, a group or a whole nation can build such a story around its past as well. Only because this could happen, however, it doesn't mean that it would result in a socially favorable outcome. Such a process can lead to polarization and not necessarily to revitalization and renewal of inter-group relations. Since a conflict process easily creates both fragmentation and narrow-mindedness, a process aimed at reversing such a mind-set needs to be diverse as well—many stories, different levels, and different ways of telling are needed in order to make the recovery of the society's image of itself a process involving as many as possible.

The idea of reconciliation, as outlined in a peace agreement, can take many shapes. Comprehensive peace agreements, as we have noted above, are today including some mechanism dealing with the past, whether through the concepts of "truth," "historical clarification" or "reception" and "reconciliation." Such mechanisms live their own life, for a shorter or longer period of time, this is part of the whole idea: reconciliation should be connected to a paradigmatic social redefinition, and if that have taken place, past should be past, and only remembered and celebrated in ordered and recognized forms, and—most important—not in the form of recurrent conflicts flaring up in an unpredictable way.

THE NEED OF JUSTICE

It should be noted here, that the introduction of truth and reconciliation commissions in recent decades have taken place in parallel with other forms which make peace processes a more profound and deep social process. The Special Panels or Courts established after many conflicts (after the conflicts in Cambodia, Rwanda, Yugoslavia, Sierra Leone, Liberia, East Timor, to mention but a few) are examples of temporary arrangements, and the ICC is the permanent mechanism established in the wake of these courts. These panels, sometimes criticized for their shortcomings, provide nevertheless a necessary corrective and challenge against the too-often practiced self-immunity of leaders of countries. The military governments in Latin America—in El Salvador, Chile, and Argentina—are good illustrations of this behavior. The legal aspect is only one of several dimensions in a more profound treatment of post-conflict issues. The political apology is an interesting example of an act where incumbent leaders find it necessary and possible to explicitly apologize for abuses in the past.

The general problem that is in focus through this development is, we can assume, as old as war itself. Also the morally most justifiable wars result in suffering and death as well as material devastation. Historically, war compensation was only paid by states to states, but the idea that individual persons should be, or have the right to be, compensated in one war or another is a relatively new one. Basically it is a recognition of the increasingly stronger place of the individual in general in the modern society, and in international legal terms including not the least the development of international human rights and human rights law. It can be seen as a recognition of the state's trespassing of a moral boundary between the state and the individual, caused by conflict behavior.

FIVE WAYS OF DEALING WITH THE PAST

In connection to the introduction of the reconciliation dimension into politics, and mainly in peace processes, we have also seen the emergence of concepts like "forgiveness," "truth," and "compensation," alongside with the more "traditional" concepts of "conflict resolution," "peace-making," "justice," and "peace." Reconciliation has also been introduced in other situations, for instance where historical justice or compensation is brought up as a political issue in its own right, and not due to a preceding ongoing conflict. To this category belongs also the recognition of historic injustices against, for instance, indigenous populations—such as in Australia, Canada, and Sweden. Also, in the discussion on the handing back of historic artifacts, to their places of origin, the idea of reconciling peoples, who may have lived in enmity over centuries, has been strengthened by a reconciliation perspective.

The concept of "reconciliation" has in its political context come to represent different types of initiatives taken against the shadow of historical injustices, for instance recognition and restoration (individual or collective), or compensation (material or symbolic). The forms for this, as well as the practical circumstances under which they are possible to realize, are by no means given or obvious. Two main reasons seem to be good explanations of this.

The first could be that each social process that brings individual experiences into the atmosphere of a society, requires time and respect for the situation of the individual person, as well as for his/her previous role in a conflict—a conflict that actually was not an individual project, but a collective one (since it was political). The situation is likely not to have improved substantially—historic reasons for a conflict are seldom sorted out in a clarifying and refreshing way, even if a peace agreement has been signed. Since each individual person lives with an internal process of moral (re)orientation, the actors on a political level can never ask for a certain pace of mental change, that everyone should join in. Instead, the political level can create spaces for each and everyone's process to be known and respected.

This does not imply, on the other hand, that the society cannot go on towards new relations and common grounds for development, but there are limits to what extent this should be based on individual acts of, for example, forgiveness.

A second reason may be, that a truth and reconciliation process—with all its intricate interests, mystified stories about the past, and deeply felt needs for a better life in general—might actually require a society that is totally different compared to what a so called post-conflict society normally is an example of. When the conditions for reconciliation are lacking—political stability, supportive and critical civil society, established judiciary, and a normative basis accepting reconciliation as a broad, social process—then we should, maybe, not expect reconciliation under such conditions to be more than partial, something that by many is regarded as a half-measure.

One can look upon these developments as new and innovative ways of dealing with a troubling past. Where some countries today are open to talk about a past that is not to their advantage in some respects, other countries still feel that this is neither appropriate nor possible to do in a way that is not threatening to them. In the following of this chapter we will look closer into ways of dealing with the past, ways that are methods of principle which countries have chosen for various reasons, at various points in time.

Reconciliation is by definition a "historically directed" concept, seeking its role and meaning in dealing with the past. However, there are many ways by which societies deal with the past, and special historic experiences may lead to very special forms of approaches, mechanisms or social taboos as a way to manage precarious historic situations. In the following we shall identify five such ways of dealing with the past. The five ways are: silence, compensation, truth and memory, meeting the other, and the legal process.

> Only when we are reconciled, court processes will be meaningful. If not they will be acts of revenge. And when reconciled, people realize the necessity of justice, and will therefore also do what is justice.

This quotation refers to one of many opinions, in discussions on justice, peace and reconciliation, in Timor Leste before and after independence 2002. It is not a unique view in that country. Issues of justice, revenge, forgiveness, and reconciliation were part of daily life, for some intensive years of conflict and peace-making at the turn of the millennium, in this small territory—a former Portuguese colony.

In the following we shall discuss reconciliation from this point of departure, beginning with the zero-level state of mind in relation to reconciliation: the silence.

Silence—The Opposite of Truth

When confronting the past, silence is in many ways more difficult to deal with, than is a lie. Silence—whether officially declared or self-imposed—works as a rejection of the past, of its existence, a denial of history one may say. Silence claims implicitly, in a context of for instance reconciliation, that there are things that do not exist anymore, and every wish to change that by bringing light to them is denied as incomprehensive and irrelevant. Silence is therefore an absolute hinder for reconciliation, in particular since reconciliation means a relation. To overcome the effects of silence, for those that nevertheless know something, is then possible only through unilateral acts—such as forgiveness. Something that—without repeating the argument above—points to the need for keeping forgiveness as a concept in its own right.

Lies are different. Lies try to escape, to flee and destroy. Such things can be confronted, revealed and truth is by that given a chance, so to say.

It takes a toll to remember difficult, hurting events. To "forget," or to suppress, is a fully understandable method to keep hard memories away. This goes for individuals as well as for communities and, for the same reason, for states. This "method of silence" is then a protection mechanism which, besides working psychologically, also fits as hand to glove for those that have other than psychological reasons to forget, for instance in order to avoid possible attention from courts, friends, or media.

One may ask whether silence has anything to do in a text about political reconciliation. There is the expression, not only in English, of being "reconciled to one's fate." This connects well to silence, since the fate is "silent." It is an external and immovable force that brings us into unknown life situations, for better or worse. To reconcile to one's fate can be done together with others, or be done as a very private acceptance of what life has come to be. Since this act of "recognition before life" for many, in particular after conflict and other violent experiences, is an active mechanism to overcome an immediate and threatening state, this process of silence has been the one and only possible life attitude for the time being.

Leaving the individual level, it needs to be said that not all public peace processes include mechanisms for truth or for reconciliation, even if the examples of the opposite are many. For instance, in the—at the time well-known—armed conflict and subsequent peace agreement between Frelimo and Renamo in Mozambique 1992, there was no truth or reconciliation component included. There have been such processes initiated locally in Mozambique since then, however, but initiated outside the public process. Often these processes have concerned the rehabilitation of child soldiers.

Leaving current developments for a moment, it should also be noted that silence is a classic, realpolitik attitude versus the commons when it comes to foreign policy. Traditionally, foreign policy has been, and still is in many places, the least transparent and democratically anchored part of a government's work, also in democracies. The national interest does not allow for a broad discussion in many questions, partly since unity has to be showed towards the outside, and partly since an open discussion can reveal how the thinking goes, and what options are discussed. A war is an affair between states, the traditional view holds, and therefore it is also ended in some kind of agreement between states. This isolation of foreign policy issues have contributed to keep issues of consequences away from the political agenda. A war was regarded, therefore, by people in general as something that one almost could not control whether "it comes" or not, almost like a serious influenza.

A case where the politics of silence towards the past has been employed, but where changes recently have taken place, is Spain. To hold back and conceal was a conscious strategy, widely accepted at the time, in order to deal with some very uncomfortable memories from the civil war (1933–1939) and the Franco period as a whole. This approach was, according to many, a method of paving the way for democracy. The same situation was at hand when Chile and Argentina in similar political situations during the 1980s and 1990s. While the military in these countries ruled about amnesty for themselves when handing over power, the countries have nevertheless had truth commissions. Spain has not, and there is today an increasingly strong opinion among the younger generation in that country about clarifying the past. Several forensic projects are going on, or have been finalized, which have brought up issues of truth and responsibility from the pre-democratic period of modern Spain. A common lesson from all three examples is that the imposed public silence did not hold for the new and democratic era that was coming.

The approach of Latin American military governments, when—for one reason or the other—leave power, namely to give themselves amnesty, is not only an easy way out for individuals who are responsible for numerous violations of human rights. As long as the military as a group holds some power—which in the end is what militaries always do, the matter is who controls it—the question is always raised in such situations whether or not a change would be possible that included responsibility on part of the perpetrators: Can skeletons in the militaries' cupboard be brought into the light at the same time as they give up their power? If so, would they give up? Should they rather be defeated in an armed confrontation, or in a prolonged civil war? Should they be lured into a complot which in the end brings them before an international court?

This is not an academic list of questions but a down-to-earth political reality that democratically minded politicians have to deal with—not only in some countries in Latin America and Europe during the 1970s, but much later in South Africa, East Timor, and Nepal, to mention a few.

Is it possible to talk about the method of silence in any positive terms if these terms would mean that a common process of interpretation, a broad search for truth and possibilities for justice and reconciliation would not be given a chance? No, that is not possible.

On the other hand, one cannot rule out that silence in a given political moment can be one of many other roads towards progress in other fields. If this silence is possible to morally legitimize is a matter for each case, but a case can be made here, that in line with the same principles and thinking, that guides a moral approach to the morally justified war, the same way of thinking should be legitimate to use in order to identify when we should accept less than perfect conditions for a morally legitimate peace. One situation is a mirror of the other.

In line with this argument follows the idea that silence as a method can be, from the very beginning, a temporary measure. The hypothesis is then, that when a society is strong enough to carry its own truth, i.e., to openly discuss also the most serious and sensitive relations between different groups, the demand for justice will as well be formulated. Those who support this thinking would point at the development in Chile and Argentina, as well as in Spain. After a few decades these countries have created the necessary institutional and political strength—"maturity"—that is necessary for raising the issues publically and legally. For the victims this may mean that—if they survived in the first place—have had a long period of non-recognition and probably prolonged suffering. For those that were killed, or have died in the period since then, their life and death will only posthumously be recognized.

Some would claim that this approach should nevertheless be the "normal procedure"—what we discuss is nothing less than nation-wide disasters and rehabilitation. Are there no institutions that could take care of perpetrators, then one will have to establish them, the claim goes. In the mean-time a less then perfect state of affairs will rule. The "quick-fix culture" of the modern, consumer society cannot be allowed to take over our way of thinking about methods and approaches, another argument goes, when it comes to individual human lives, collective stories about suffering and the formation of a new vision of the future.

South Africa, with its national unity government created in the most critical transitional period, is again an interesting and deviating example, since the country at the beginning of this period had a functioning legal system—a judiciary, a police, and a parliament that could legislate—something that most states are missing after internal armed conflicts. Although parts of that system had been serving and in a way represented the apartheid system, and therefore also committed many of its crimes, it was not rejected out of hand as a system for this reason. In other countries, there were but a remnant of a former judiciary, when the peace finally came, such as in Sierra Leone, Liberia, and East Timor. Through international assistance legal and legislative institutions were developed, often physically built as well as internally developed, through capacity training in administration, legal training and security systems reform in general. In the meantime, internationally manned courts or special panels were set up in order to deal with some of the perpetrators of serious crimes. In the end, no country is stronger than its own legal system—that's the main argument from those that hold this view on how to deal with violators of justice during war and dictatorship.

When countries—such as Chile, Argentina, and Spain, just to keep on to these examples—show that it doesn't mean neither social break-down nor a political revolution to allow information that is embarrassing or outright accusative for power-holders or prominent persons. Instead, this gives hope for anyone being a victim. The psychological importance on the individual level of bringing hard and suppressed experiences into light is a very good example in the case of sexual abuse within the Catholic Church.

We have seen that silence as a psychological phenomenon in some instances may work hand in hand with a political inclination on part of those potentially accused, since both will make life less troublesome. It takes a toll to share hurting information. Whether or not silence is employed—as a self-imposed or officially proclaimed attitude—a parliament or other institution has always the possibility in a future to revise and return to what once was buried. There is no political or legal safety mechanism for violators. A new generation can make new priorities. As long as silence is functioning, then, it does not serve the purpose for which reconciliation is employed or developed. It cannot be but a morally intricate side-step, at best legitimized by its achievement and not by its nature. For that reason we leave this method here. It is only when silence is replaced by something that moves the reality—not necessarily a complete truth, as we have noted—that a reconciliation process can be developed.

Truth—The Basis

In order for reconciliation to develop, for instance in a direction towards compensation or prosecution, truth has to be given a central place: in relation to identified persons, specific information needs to be collected in an as comprehensive and factual way as possible. In this work, there is a dimension of truth, as the concept is regarded by courts as well as by many truth and reconciliation commissions. Some commissions have been focused on this aspect of truth, and often been successful in this. In El Salvador the information about persecutors was specific and clear, names and their participation was identified. Later, this level of information was deemed too detailed in the neighboring country Guatemala, when a commission should do the same type of analysis. In East Timor, the commission's strong side was its ability to bring out information about events that were not at all described before. The report of the commission with its over 3,000 pages tells a story that can never be ignored. East Timor was occupied by Indonesia during the same period, mainly, as was investigated by its truth and reconciliation commission. Thus, a lot of events that relate to Indonesia's role were explained by the commission, events that otherwise most probably would have been left for disappearing with history.

RECONCILIATION AS POLITICS

Views vary among international organizations, be they non-governmental or government organizations. The "truth"—with its different meanings recognized is the overarching dimension that all involved would support unequivocally as a critical aspect of any social and/or legal process.

As a continuation of the process of mourning and interpreting the past—irrespective of whether a psychological or legal variant of this process is employed—there is an often expressed need for survivors, relatives and others to be able to settle, in order to continue. Many countries find a form to remember on the collective level. Rwanda, Perú, and East Timor are all building monuments for remembrance.

There is an important distinction to be made between the individual and the society when it comes to dealing with the truth that one has been able to establish. Naturally, the individual person asks the question: what do I do with what I know? An individual has the right to do what he/she wants—forget, reconcile, dig deeper, whatever. An individual has the right to say that "I know, but I want to leave it behind. History is history, I cannot be a victim of the past, in my life orientation." Nobody should be forced to remember, one can say.

A society, however, cannot argue in the same way. It has a duty to remember, in order not to forget but to learn from, and be reminded about, its own history. One can see the different forms of memorialization that societies undertake as a bridge between the individual and the collective.

The right to the truth, interpreted as the right to know conditions that concern oneself is a human right of relevance in many situations—in particular when issues of life, freedom, and death are at stake. The truth dimension is one of the most effective tools for the defense of human rights in post-conflict societies since its implications are wide, far beyond the right to know what happened—it builds a basis for both justice and equality.

Compensation

To compensate, most often materially, has been a way of showing recognition and respect for suffering, discrimination and other forms of illegal or unjust treatment—a respect expressed by a new era, a new government. There are probably many more such commissions working than is generally known, foremost they have been working with claims for damages, such as in Switzerland (Jewish assets confiscated during the Second World War), Brazil (during the military dictatorship period), or in Morocco or Northern

Ireland. In this context those commissions that work in relation to a conflict or dictatorship period fit best into the discussion here. The various problems that arise in any compensation situation—for what, how, and how much?—often leads to generalized decisions, in practice a symbolic recognition more than compensation in the sense of an attempt to meet the material costs that have been incurred in the past. Also, truth commissions may have the responsibility to address compensation issues. The South African commission, again, had this mandate. The implementation of this aspect of the commission's work has been the weakest according to some analysts.

In East Timor, a reflection was made by Xanana Gusmão in relation to the phenomenon of compensation. There have been four veteran organizations in the country, organizing former guerilla soldiers, and various forms of compensation, and pensions, have been paid since independence in 2002. The prime minister has often referred to his people as heroes, but, if all are compensated, are they then also heroes? I interpreted his reflection in this way. Is it possible to talk about being a hero if you are fully compensated? Isn't it more like an insurance business, that you are sorting out with your insurance company, than a personal?

Summarizing this theme we have noted that compensation can be both individual and collective, both direct and material, as well as symbolic and indirect. A final observation that is interesting is that there are diffusion effects sometimes observed from what was intended as a compensation commission, with a relatively limited purpose and mandate, into a de facto working process with wider and more truth oriented expressions than was conceived of initially. Brazil is a case in point for such a development.

The Legal Process—A Form of Responsibility

In the period after the Second World War, a number of temporary courts have been established in order to regulate, as far as the available legal ground allowed, war crimes and comparable atrocities committed during a war. This led to some different types of legal processes where the most visible are the multi-year processes, from the Nüremburg trials in the 1940s to today's processes in Arusha (on Rwanda), Cambodia (the Khmer Rouge), and those in the Hague (post-Yugoslavia processes). But a large number of special panels—that is smaller courts with international and local staffing, dealing with relatively minor conflicts for shorter periods, such as in Sierra Leone or Timor Leste.

As has been mentioned above, there is since 2002 the ICC, which is a permanent international court dealing with war crimes and crimes against humanity as described in its founding document, the Charter of Rome. The Charter was ratified by the signatory states during 2002 to the extent that it came into force and for that reason, the ICC is able to deal with cases originating from July 1, 2002, and onwards.

These are all examples of the gravest and often most politically charged court processes over political matters in our time. Their role for national reconciliation is always difficult to measure, but a common argument about the relation between processes around a small number of previous power holders and a national reconciliation process of today is that "if the big fish never meets justice, why should then the people as a whole ever contemplate to oversee with justice in the name of reconciliation?"

In this context it is worth noting that the concept of "reconciliation" is not included in the Charter of Rome. The concept seems to be difficult to link to, or include in, any legally or otherwise theoretically meaningful way into a legal argument. Maybe this is so because of its wide scope in time. This is illustrated by the UN Security Council which in its resolution no. 1329 on the courts for former Yugoslavia and Rwanda, respectively, by saying that their work contributes to national reconciliation—a long-term vision and hope.

It should be noted at this point, that the legal dimension of a reconciliation process has many parts in common with the other forms of dealing with the past discussed in this chapter, as well as with reconciliation as defined in this book as well. One of these parts is access to "facts," to information. This is maybe the most important one, but the participation of both sides for a successful outcome, the well-balanced assessment of motives, and the conditions and requirements of a given situation, are other examples as well. Another similarity is the compensation aspect, something which is a common aspect in a court's deliberations also within a given case. However, for the ICC this is regulated in an institutionalized way, in that the Rome Charter has a mechanism for compensation ("reparation") which makes it an integrated component of the work of the ICC.

On the other side, certain things are clearly different. From a legal point of view it is, naturally enough, the legality of the matter which directs the selection and nature of facts and information included in the process.

While legality is not a narrow concept as such, it directs what is relevant, since it points at the basis for the court's mandate. This is important to remember by those that criticize courts for excluding certain dimensions, or not bringing in "all sides," or "all factors." Many persons, often with strong memories and experiences from a civil war, for instance, may see a lot of factors as relevant and important for a certain case, and, as a normal human need, want to see a wider explanation and assessment of a social process or a particular event than a court is able to give.

These interpretations, however, can emerge from the work of truth commissions, as well as from literary and other artistic products stemming out of first-hand experiences. Even today, the Second World War, the Vietnam War, the Balkan wars as well as Rwanda and the many internal wars in Latin America—all are the milieus of numerous stories of sometimes true life stories. More exciting and human than any court proceeding ever can be.

There has been a discussion about the possibility to compose international courts in way that is relevant for reconciliation processes: Do they know local conditions sufficiently well? Can they avoid the local political game and therefore continue to be relevant? What is sometimes forgotten in this debate is that even if there is a strong internal culture which in principle is ready to deal with even serious crimes, there is not necessarily a contradiction between the two. There may very well be a complementarity between local and international systems.

The Meeting

Maybe the most spectacular and widely spread part of political reconciliation processes is probably the public hearing and public meetings where the victim and the perpetrator play a public role. From South Africa we could see public events of this type in a large number. Hearings are, one must say, a standard operational procedure for truth commissions because of their information- and truth dimension. In addition, the mere articulation of what has happened, including graphic descriptions of serious crimes, means that it will never be possible in the future to argue that this did never happen or that things have been exaggerated etc. "in the light of history."

The meeting between two individuals is the event most descriptive and clear when it comes to identifying which conditions that might be a contribution of "political reconciliation" to a political process where individuals and/or groups redefine their relations into a process towards a more peaceful and dignified relationship. This is so, because a meeting between individuals, which is different from other social meetings, and which can be labeled as a reconciliatory meeting is likely to have at least three dimensions clearly at hand.

The critical dimensions in both the reconciliatory personal meeting and, I would claim, in political reconciliation as a whole in this study, are the following:

- *the principle of mutuality*. Its operational activity is the recognition of both sides, that the other side's story, life-story, is a necessary story also for "me" to understand myself fully. This is a key mechanism for redefining previously polarized relations.
- *the principle of compensation*. This mechanism in the reconciliation process follows as a natural, or logical if you will, consequence of the initial recognition: if someone, whose story is important for "me," it is not logical or natural to let things continue to be asymmetric—whatever that means: oppressive, exploitative, discriminating, or derogatory.
- *the principle of non-repetition*. This means that any repetition of the past would entail a reduction of the possibility to live a fuller life, besides all its material costs. Hurting one side would mean hurting the other.

Because of the recognition of the Other as a significant part of "my own life story," a new perspective is created on the total situation, because a new empirical reality is taken into consideration, besides the emotional and social dimensions already there. This implies that the asymmetric status between the two parties does not reflect the principle of recognition: therefore compensation (in some form) is necessary. From this second principle follows the third one, on the basis of the same logic: the past should never be allowed to repeat itself, because hurting the Other implies "hurting myself."

The principle of non-repetition is in one way the most difficult to implement, and it may actually only be possible to secure in a meaningful way through the full implementation of the two previous principles. There is however no theoretical relationship between the three principles that makes this a necessary conclusion, but it is a good hypothesis, about the interplay of the necessary social and political circumstances, that leads to this conclusion.

There is no claim for, a formal need for, individual forgiveness in the three principles above. The critical point is, as was mentioned, that recognition of the Other's life story as a necessary component for creating a meaningful one for "myself." What happens to people's mind, when they take on this perspective is the point of departure for political reconciliation.

It may very well be the case, that when the three principles above are applied, individuals will also continue and forgive each other. The opposite is possible as well—from forgiveness may come a process like the one of reconciliation. This is most probably something to rejoice and be happy for, but it is not a necessary component of the (political) reconciliation process.

Any society involved in internal armed conflict will experience polarizations and tensions between groups as a result of the conflict. There is less and less room for views and ideas from "the other side"—in media, in conversations, and among circles of friends. It is not uncommon, in particular in protracted conflicts, that persons living in one, maybe relatively peaceful part of a country, have no idea at all about what it means to be living in another part of the country—this is in particular true for areas with separation walls between areas, whether concrete or invisible—but very real.

The variation of the theme of reconciliation that the five methods of dealing with the past are describing are all components in a process that in the end may very well lead up to political reconciliation on a group or individual level.

A RELATIONSHIP?

If we make an exception for "silence" as a method (it is a "pre-truth" method, one could say) the remaining four methods, or approaches, represent a very logical order of initiatives. It seems that they would appear in the following order if listed according to their functionality: first "truth," then "responsibility," followed by "compensation" and lastly the "meeting."

This relationship can be illustrated as in Figure 4. Its arrow, pointing in two directions, illustrates that a political reconciliation process can take two routes. It can begin with top leaders, such as in South Africa, and pass on to broader groups, or vice versa, it can begin as a popular movement "forcing" leaders to take on a deeply felt need to come to terms with the past, as in the cases of apologies towards indigenous populations and rectification of historic injustices.

RECONCILIATION AS POLITICS

The figure illustrates that without truth, no responsibility and no compensation. And no meeting either—reconciliation has to be based on an understanding of what there is to be reconciled. This is, by the way, a difference from forgiveness which due to its unilateral character can be referring to whatever is in the mind of the forgiving person.

There are examples of processes that fit each of the steps in the Figure. In Guatemala, only the truth was collected as a public process after the years of military and authoritarian regimes in the 1990s. In the truth and friendship commission between Indonesia and Timor Leste, only the truth and the responsibility for the events were identified, but no compensation was paid. In Brazil, truth and responsibility (the state's) was the basis for claims for compensation of losses of families and individuals during the period of military dictatorship in the 1970s. And in South Africa, to mention just one well-known example—all four levels of the process were realized.

Figure 4. Four elements in a political reconciliation process

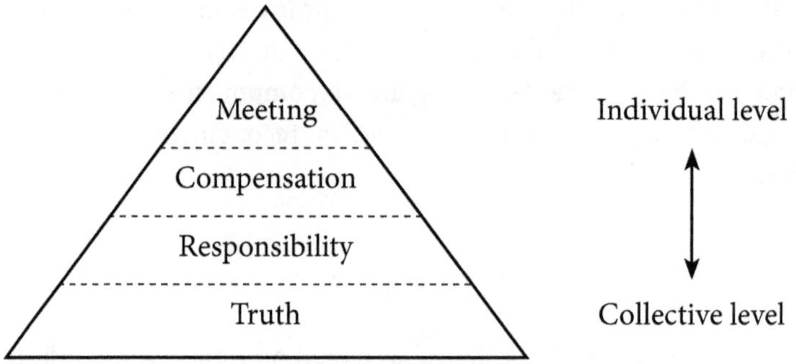

Triangle diagram with four horizontal levels from top to bottom: Meeting, Compensation, Responsibility, Truth. To the right, a vertical double-headed arrow between "Individual level" (top) and "Collective level" (bottom).

A REFLECTION

Even if there are examples of comprehensive peace processes, with many or all elements of political reconciliation, it is very difficult for some societies to reach that ideal. And one may wonder if too idealistic concepts really have a role to play in a reality struggling with its own inner contradictions. The risk under such circumstances is, that all the problems are swept under the carpet, for strategic or political or other reasons. Maybe someone thinks that if we all forgave each other, everything will be fine.

This would however be to move from one side of the road to the other. It is probably enough to accept the foundation stone of political reconciliation as understood here: the recognition of the role of the Other, for understanding oneself. On that basis, minor, small steps can be taken on, on a local or regional level (it doesn't have to be national) towards political reconciliation. That is not a costly initiative in material terms, but much more so politically and from a human point of view.

In order to assist in avoiding the two extremes, the concept of reconciliation in a political context needs to be given a fairly specific content so that it can be identified and realized. One doesn't have to be friends, or forgive, or forget, or do similar things, but instead integrate the Other as part of a larger image of oneself. This creates the consequence that hurting the Other means hurting oneself. The suffering of the Other means the suffering of someone important to oneself. Discrimination against the Other means that my own history is discriminated against. These are all relation-building components which do not require a specific political view, religious belief or ethnic identity. This is a relevant point in this context, since we are trying to create conditions for reconciliation.

4

A Structural Theory of Reconciliation

The concept of reconciliation is not only a concept that has found its way from arenas outside "politics" but, we claim here, is in itself a political concept as well. It influences, and is in certain situations capable of explaining, the distribution of moral claims and power of individuals and groups in contest over power issues, in a society.

For many political actors, the concept of reconciliation has become a conceptual target for post-conflict processes—distant but somehow, and nevertheless, a point of reference. For instance, when the Secretary-General of the United Nations in different documents expresses why transitional justice is a necessary part of the work of the international community, the possibility for reconciliation is mentioned as one of several distant goals, such as justice and peace.[1] Reconciliation—whatever it means in a UN context—is in these documents something emerging in a longer perspective and therefore it is not possible to reach through a process that from the beginning has to be limited in time and space—such as a court process, or a truth commission's work, to mention two examples.

This is a somewhat aloof approach to reconciliation in politics, according to some parties and actors in conflicts and wars, in particular by groups whose rights are directly or indirectly violated. Also among those parties who are directly negotiating an agreement of some sort realize, that the truth dimension, and as a prolongation of that the questions of justice and reconciliation, is not possible to avoid anymore. All major agreements, as we have noted in other chapters, are today including a truth component

---

1. See for instance United Nations, *Report*; United Nations, *Guidance Note*.

in one way or another. It is not only a matter of truth as such, but of legitimacy in the eyes of the wider population, on behalf of the parties.

Thus, the question of truth and reconciliation is certainly raised, after serious crimes and violations of human rights have been committed in armed conflicts and wars. It is raised by large numbers of civilians—often representing themselves individually as victims or by civil society organizations—but the international community has limited possibilities on the formal level to take on their demands and claims. In between the individuals and the international community are the states, who as well have suffered from civil war and which try in one way or another, with or without serious ambitions, to manage their own past on the basis of available resources—human and material.

Such a situation contains a number of not only individual dimensions—which is often in focus when human rights are discussed—but also some structural conditions which actually set the parameters for what is, and what may not be, possible to do. For that reason we shall make some basic observations on the relationship between social structures as conditions for political reconciliation.

RECONCILIATION IS CONDITIONAL FORGIVENESS?

When kept on a distance, the presence of the reconciliation dimension in peace processes is maybe causing strategic moves by the parties. But when it is getting closer to realization, the compulsory reflection is immediately there: on what conditions? A spontaneous response from persons with a fundamental human or humanistic view of life would be to say, that reconciliation is—almost by definition—without conditions. It is and should be unconditional. This is the point with reconciliation, some would say. It seems, at this point of the argument, that we have now left the political sphere: can anything in politics be meaningful if it is realized without conditions, without criteria for its realization?

We shall keep this issue burning for a little while and further analyze the conditionality aspect and also keep the seemingly close relationship between "reconciliation" and "forgiveness," analyzed in a previous chapter, but relevant also here.

Let us take a look at the South African truth and reconciliation process during the 1990s as an example. In South Africa, at the time, "reconciliation" was conditioned in the sense that only those that shared the truth about their acts during the Apartheid period could be considered for amnesty. If this did not happen, the regular court system was supposed to take care of the legal aspects of a person's Apartheid legacy. This was a core exchange in the nation-wide process of reconciliation. Information, then, was seen not only as of value for the general national history of South Africa but equally important for the individual history of persons, and their families, suffering from the Apartheid years.

Back to reconciliation and forgiveness. Many texts and speeches about reconciliation in politics are bordering to mix the concept up with forgiveness, that is, to be about the individual person's capacity to put aside, and for the future give up the possibility of giving moral weight to a defined hurting past. Many books have been written on this theme, and Archbishop Desmond Tutu[2] is an excellent case in point.

In this context there is one aspect in the nature of forgiveness that is important. Let us repeat for a second what was mentioned briefly above, namely that a person may forgive another one, also without the other person's knowledge. The quality or sincerity of forgiveness is not dependent on the knowledge about it, of the person, or group, which is forgiven. Thus, also a person who is not alive can be totally forgiven, for that reason. Forgiveness is then a conviction, about what is right and good to do, of the forgiving person. As we have seen, forgiveness has the characteristics of a gift—an unconditional unilateral act conveying a positive message/content from one person to another.

Let us compare this with the nature of reconciliation. There is one immediate and important difference—reconciliation cannot be a "surprise," it is a relationship. Two persons, or two peoples, that are reconciling are aware of what is going on, it is a relationship-building process, where reconciliation is the name for both the process and the goal. To reconcile is to build a relation, the concept is *relational*. Forgiveness, however, is a *unilateral* concept.

At this point we need to say, that while this is a theoretical differentiation of the concepts, the reality very often is, that if forgiveness or reconciliation is at all "on the agenda," actors or victims (or people in general) would both forgive and reconcile with each other, and nobody would care about the distinction.

So why would we then be concerned with a distinction between forgiveness and reconciliation? The main reason is, that the perspective of

---

2. Tutu, *No Future*.

reconciliation is and should be a political perspective and that is by definition different from the interpersonal level. We are concerned about the community level of social relations, of what is common in a society. For that reason, a relational concept is likely to be much better equipped to describe and explain what may happen in a society then is a unilateral one. If we make forgiveness a common, in some situations natural component, we are close to make forgiveness a condition for political development. Anyone stating that we need to forgive so that the peace process can go on would impose a new burden on people. Forgiveness should remain anchored in the heart of the individual and not in a political process. It benefits from being dependent on the individual's private psychological and social capacity to deal with the past. The respect for the individual's integrity requires that pressure to forgive or reconcile should never be the result of a political process.

This should of course not stop any government's attempts to plan for making space for reconciliation. This is instead exactly what governments and, when appropriate, the international community, should do: create forums, platforms in different types of media, establish mechanisms for sharing, investigating, discussing, and analyzing the past and thereby allow people to come forward, to share, and compare their own experiences with those of others.

The conclusion is then, from this argument, that forgiveness is a concept that should be left outside the political arena. This is so because of its genuinely private, and sometimes intimate, character. In this era of expositions of the inner life of the individual we should spare some words for that part of life, and not "politicize" the concept of forgiveness through the back-door of political reconciliation.

In addition to this we should note, that forgiveness, as a concept, does not include a dimension of "future" or "reconstruction" or "community." In fact, the point with forgiveness is to deal specifically with the past, and not the future. It is a strength of the concept of forgiveness not to deal with the future, since the future can never be fully controlled (and maybe not forgiven) and—put in an optimistic tone—the future may be positively affected by forgiveness of the past. Therefore, let forgiveness stay with the past, even if it means an act of forgiveness every evening!

The effect of forgiveness is just like reconciliation something for the future to experience. They both opens new roads towards the future, they

RECONCILIATION AS POLITICS

create a different basis for the future but do it from two different perspective—the individual and the political, respectively.

RECONCILIATION—ASPECTS OF BOTTOM-UP AND TOP-DOWN APPROACHES

Post-conflict reconciliation processes, in order to be effective, are one of the best examples of how necessary it is to combine bottom-up and top-down approaches to peace building.

If we start with the top-down process, and look at some experiences, one dimension turns out to be critical: the attitude of the winning side towards its own history. It is a strong hypothesis, that there is a relationship between a leadership's—a government's—willingness to acknowledge its mistakes in the past and other parties' willingness to do the same thing.

Armed conflicts are to a large extent elite projects, without material resources an armed conflict cannot continue over time. Rebellions, upheavals, mutiny, looting, burnings, killings—there are many ways by which non-armed but still very violent actions can take place. The armed conflict, however, requires weapons, training, and communication. Thus, settlement of armed conflicts requires dealing with these elites—militarily crushed or not, they represent access to resources that can either spoil an agreement or support and strengthen it. The elite's way of dealing with reconciliation—being it against or in line with their personal will—is critical, due to the resources the elites' by definition can control.

A much debated apology during a reconciliation process was in South Africa made by its former president de Klerk to the South African Truth and Reconciliation Commission, where he said that:

> Apartheid was wrong. I apologize in my capacity as leader of the National Party to the millions of South Africans who suffered the wretched disruption of forced removals in respect of their homes, businesses and land. Who over the years suffered the shame of being arrested for pass law offences. Who over the decades and indeed centuries suffered the indignities and humiliation of racial discrimination.[3]

So far the top-down perspective. The bottom-up perspective establishes the peace and reconciliation process among those that have suffered the

---

3. Huyse, "Offenders," 73.

most—the direct victims, the general population, the internally displaced, etc. It is easier said than done, to integrate broad layers of a population—in a country torn by war and divisions—into a process where most, at least, feel involved or at least have access to the extent wanted. Even well-functioning information based countries can yet have problems with such tasks. The moral and political reasons pointing at the necessity to bring all groups in do not make it practically easier. However, they give good reasons for letting this process *take its time*. This is the only solution to the commitment idea: lack of resources can be compensated by time, a resource that a peace process should have plenty of!

STRUCTURE AND RECONCILIATION

Political reconciliation has been defined in another chapter as a process where a) relations are established where "the other's story" is recognized as a necessary component for "my story" to be complete, and where b) harm, that come from the inability to see this need, should be repaired, and where c) it is agreed that such a situation should never be allowed to take form again.

This definition illustrates how political reconciliation is a virtual opposite to characteristics of a political conflict. Such a conflict is driven by, and resulting in, increased polarization; creating harm is seen as a mover of the parties' own interests and opinions and they like to see this behavior as morally legitimate. Compare this to "political reconciliation" where depolarization, recognition, and repairing for harm are the key concepts and there is a stark difference. And—it can be noted here—forgiveness is not mentioned in the reconciliation definition.

Normally, processes of truth and reconciliation in a political context have been conceptualized as national projects. They have been intended to include "all" and to cover a historic period on both local and national levels. The projects have been announced as non-political and pursued during a fairly short period of time, when a committed and intensive work should be carried out, preferably by all citizens in a way that is corresponding to their individual levels of involvement in the conflict under scrutiny.

In some processes, however, some groups have committed themselves more than other to truth and reconciliation processes. Maybe it is not difficult to understand why it can be like that. In South Africa, again, the whites have been criticized as a group, as well as a number of Apartheid political figures, for not coming forward in the reconciliation process to the extent and with the commitment showed by many black leaders. In the same way, those who were victorious in the East Timor referendum on its international status were criticized by the losing side for not realizing that also violations in the name of a liberation struggle may need to be sorted out also morally, if confidence should be established on a deeper level in a society. Briefly stated: not only the "loser's violence" needs to be scrutinized, but also the "winner's."

Actually, the two cases of South Africa and East Timor—today the Democratic Republic of Timor Leste—illustrate to structurally very different situations. In South Africa it was the reactions of the well-off elite, the previous holders of political power, that shines through in their attitude to reconciliation. A common reaction was: Why ever bother if you can escape from responsibility by being silent? The conclusion may be, that their strong economic or political situation did not protect against a fundamental change of the society they had created.

Also in East Timor the economically strongest group was not successful in the UN popular consultation over the country's future in 1999. The more nationalistic but economically weaker groups were capable of maintaining their traditionally strong position among people in general for a self-determination process through referendum. The outcome of the two political processes—the fall of Apartheid and the fall of Indonesian occupation—was a victory for the structurally weakest groups in South Africa and East Timor, respectively.

This historic experience indicates that a too simple understanding of structural theory arguments, saying that economic and social structure will ultimately decide the outcome of major political processes, will have to be revised. Let us take on the task here.

We will then consider two structurally different types of political reconciliation processes: horizontal and vertical political reconciliation, respectively. *Horizontal* reconciliation is then a process between equals, ideally equals in all dimensions relevant to the process, such as experiences, resources, political roles, number of people involved etc. In real life we can think of guerilla groups, or political organizations, civil society groups, religious organizations and the like, as possible examples of organizations that can get involved in horizontal political reconciliation.

Vertical political reconciliation, then, is a process between un-equals— in terms of economy, insight/knowledge, force capacity and the like. Typical examples are reconciliation processes where a political leadership meets a discriminated group, where an army general apologizes for having put soldiers before unnecessary risks, or where a government apologizes for atrocities in wartime against other peoples.

Such a dichotomy is not only of academic interest. Many in South Africa gave air to the view that if white leaders of the past had no interest in viewing the blacks as a vital and respected part of a future South Africa, why should then a black person reassess personal judgments about the white policeman who battled black demonstrators into broken bodies in demonstrations in the past? In other words: the possibility of horizontal reconciliation (policeman—demonstrator) is related to the vertical (leader—people) relation, and if the vertical one is not restored there is no moral reason for restoring the horizontal. What actually happened in South Africa according to some was that the strong leadership of the black civil society, not the least through the moral force of Archbishop Tutu, more or less enforced the few acknowledgements of misuse of power from the white leadership that there were.

Also those black economic elites that benefitted from the Apartheid system had to come to terms with their past in the wake of nation-wide political reconciliation. This became clear particularly in Ciskei, Kwazulu, and Bophupatswana. Elite groups were simply forced to re-interpret, or rather reassess, their involvement with the Apartheid system. The challenge for the white leadership was not only to meet their black counter-parts and acknowledge their special role for the future of the whites (horizontal reconciliation) but also to explain why they gave up on Apartheid in front of the thousands of the white security and police men who had put their life at risk for a suddenly abandoned system, but also they had—if they wanted to reconcile politically—to reach out to the black majority with their message of a changed attitude to Apartheid (vertical reconciliation). The opposite relationship was also clear: in what way could a black leader convince a white grass-roots movement about his sincere will of maintaining a South Africa inclusive of whites also in the future? That would be an act in vertical reconciliation crossing double structural barriers: economic status and color.

South Africa represents here, for illustrative purposes, a good example of the problematique that a structural analysis of political reconciliation brings up. At the same time, when analyzing South Africa, almost anything can be written without reference to the Apartheid impact, which may give an impression of an "over-polarization" of the country and reduces comparability with other countries experiences of post-conflict reconstruction.

SOME CONCLUSIONS FOR THEORIZING

On the basis of these rather indicative arguments, we shall look into the question under what conditions a structure, that is lasting characteristics of relations between individuals or groups in a given society, is a central part of making political reconciliation effective and/or functional and if it is possible to legitimate.

Let us then summarize the conditions for the likelihood of effective political reconciliation so far:

- in a society with a strong moral asymmetry between groups
- when other mechanisms in a society are not at hand for restoring this asymmetry
- when alternative approaches, including in-action, most probably would create increased polarization or tension than a serious attempt at reconciliation would do, and
- when there are reasonably good conditions for improving the future situation towards a more morally symmetric relationship between groups, through a reconciliation process.

It is possible to describe the process as in Table 4.

Table 4. Differences between conflict relation and reconciled relation

	Conflict relation	Reconciled relation
The perpetrator	Denial;	Acknowledgement;
	Dominance;	Democracy
	Exploitation	
The Other (the victim)	Isolation;	Recognition;
	Submission;	Empowerment;
	Poverty	Development

So far this process is horizontal: structurally equal parties that reconcile. Under such conditions, parties who have at least a tacit agreement about reconciling, can develop a strong sense of personal affinity and togetherness— "brothers in (formerly antagonistic) arms." This is so since they share many experiences, they are professional, and they may even have fought each other at certain points and share the luck of surviving. It is not unusual that both sides share the idiosyncracies that have shaped their fate in life and they may therefore also share a degree of criticism against their leaders. If this is an elite experience, it is not necessarily typical. Palestinian and Israeli youth, as well as young people from the Catholic and Protestant communities in Northern Ireland, to take just two out of large numbers, have done the same type of experiences when meeting and learning about each other.

Horizontal reconciliation is both theoretically and, most likely, practically more easy to realize. But what about vertical reconciliation? This is particularly tricky when it is not only within one's own camp, but a process with the other side, the conflicting camp. For instance, in what way can Palestinian civilians, living for instance in Gaza or the West Bank, be reconciled with Israeli political leaders in case of a peace agreement? What actions would be needed from both sides to reach that level of relationship? And, likewise, what would be needed for a Palestinian leader to do, in order to reach a level of reconciled relations with the Israeli society at large? What is illustrated here is the double problem of reaching out beyond one's own status level, and one's own side as well, in the conflict. Of course, it is not an easy thing to do.

In light of the analysis, so far, it is possible to formulate two propositions on the structural impact on political reconciliation, and say that:

1. in horizontal reconciliation processes, relations between the parties would benefit from being understood through terms describing the process as inter-personal relations (trust, recognition, mutuality)

2. in vertical reconciliation processes, relations between the parties would benefit from being understood through terms describing the process as structural (justice, reparation, inclusion).

While trust and recognition as stated and practiced attitudes would be a type of outcome of reconciliation according to the first proposition, justice and inclusion in a society, through concrete social changes, would be the tool of reconciliation according to the second proposition. Thus, and in short, structure creates conditions which set the limits for what type of political reconciliation is possible.

In the horizontal reconciliation process there is through the structural similarities an overlapping basis of common interests between the parties. Mediators in conflicts are experts in utilizing this common basis—a common basis that parties benefit from and take for granted if and when they are not in conflict (for other reasons) between each other.

In the vertical type of reconciliation, on the other hand, the lack of personally overlapping interests between the groups need to be compensated through structures that are created. These structures should create predictability and content in the development of the relations between the two sides, and thus in the long run they may be able to convey both results on ground and a change in attitudes and increased trust between the two sides. Thus structural mechanisms can overcome structural barriers.

Finally, there is always an interplay between the individual person and social structures. Some individuals can through their personal capacity change structures to the better, if their ideas are followed up and made real. Also vice versa is true: good structures can make bad leadership less influential than it would otherwise have been. Since reconciliation is no exception, or free zone from structural impact, we need to include these dimensions in a deepened understanding of the structural dimension of political reconciliation.

5

Human Rights and Peace-Building

Human rights and peace-building represent two distinct theoretical approaches to the human condition, often developed in an interplay between research and politics. Each one has its own background, distinctive features, and key dimensions. Nevertheless they have a number of dimensions in common. They deal with the relation between the individual and society, they both relate to institutional dimensions of society, and they indicate how human dignity could be realized in this world. At the same time, they are very disparate perspectives—one is based on interstate agreements, gradually are taking shape as national legislation, the other one is a political process that tries to establish and secure peace by peaceful means.

A key matter is of course, whether or not human rights and peace are so intertwined that it does not make sense theoretically, to make a distinction between them? Some would claim that the implementation of human rights is conducive to peace, and peace, in its turn, is a pre-requisite for human rights implementation. In addition to this double causality, some would argue that the status of peace as a human right is generally clear: "We the inhabitants of the earth, do have a right to peace, and since this is a right for all "peoples," then by definition it is a universal human right."[1] This position is criticized by Jack Donnelly who argues that peace in this sense is a collective right, and that it does not automatically extend itself into an individual right—no matter how attractive the idea might be.[2] Rights require per definition someone responsible for their realization, and both examples

---

1. Said and Lerche, "Peace as a Human Right," 130.
2. Donnelly, *International Human Rights*.

rest on the problem of creating a duty bearer of a particular individual right to, for instance, peace or love—or both.

For the purpose of this chapter, we will accept Donnelly's argument, that peace as such is not an individual human right, but at the same time it needs to be stated—what is commonly accepted—that human rights are a feature of peace, while at the same time it is true that some rights can be enjoyed also in wartime, and, at the other end of the line, some others are definitively violated during war, or as a consequence of war.

A fundamental difference in the nature of human rights and peace-building lies in the fact that human rights have an individual approach (to human security), while peace-building almost per definition—since "peace" is understood as a state of society—is a collective effort. This difference has wide implications for the policy and practice of creating security in a society, at any given point in time.

One such implication, to which we also will return later, is visible in weak, post-conflict societies in the process of rebuilding their social and political "infra-structure." In such situations, "peace organizations" often argue for collective solutions to security problems, relating them to dialogue, reconciliation, reconstruction, and collective reparation. For "human rights organizations," on the other hand, the individual responsibility and its legal foundation and personal implications—both for the victim and the perpetrator—are key features of the reconstruction of security in such a society. In concrete situations, in particular societies with scarce resources, these differences can imply dilemmas for practitioners and politicians alike, who are advised very different approaches, depending on to whom they listen.

There is of course a wider scope of application, both of the human rights perspective and peace-building, then this example. For instance, human rights has—relatively speaking—recently become a tool for both defining and motivating development cooperation. Although this approach does have its particular emphases, it sometimes has a lot in common with peace-building efforts in similar communities or situations. One uniting aspect is often the institution-building aspect, together with conflict prevention.

THE HUMANITARIAN FAMILY

Human rights and peace-building are deeply practical and political fields, besides their formal institutionalization through, for instance, a legal and/or constitutional system of a state. While the legality—or worse: legalism—of the human rights system is a matter of institutionalization and formalization of what initially is a moral and ethical principle, also peace-building seeks the institutionalization of its moral principles so as to make any arbitrary application of decision-making procedures, or coup-d'état-like actions, virtually impossible to undertake.

The Human Rights and Peace-Building discourses are easily identified as carriers of a number of common principles of dignity, rights, righteousness, and justice. Both of them represent an ambition on part of the international community—whatever that concept means—to secure peace, justice and development in the deepest sense. This may require action in the midst of high-level violence/war, or as part of transitions from one political system to another, as well as during a long-term and slow process of small but visible steps towards improved life conditions under peace-time conditions.

On the other hand, the two discourses represent traditions that have developed their respective discourses under different conditions and historical circumstances. While for instance the emergence of the Red Cross/Crescent Movement, over a century ago now, plus the result of innumerable international conferences represent a combination of an, over the years, increasingly legally based humanitarianism, the peace-building community of organizations and movements has its roots either in a historic pacifism and critique against violence and militarism as phenomena, or from periods of reaction against threatening developments, such as the atomic bomb, nuclear deterrence, the arms trade or an increased general militarization of society.

This chapter addresses, and tries to develop, some conceptual approaches, for the analysis of issues currently discussed in the overlapping field of human rights and peace-building.

"Peace-building" refers here to a social process which reduces the level of violence as behavior or as mentality ("militarism") in a society, with the purpose of establishing long-term non-violent group relations, incl. mechanisms for conflict management and/or resolution. Thus we are linking relevant human rights provisions to such processes in this section.

RECONCILIATION AS POLITICS

We should as well remind ourselves about the conflict triangle's both simple but useful concepts: the (destructive) *behavior*, the *attitudes* of the parties, and their *incompatible* positions. One point with these is, that social conflict could escalate as well as de-escalate through a process of mutually reinforcement between the three corners. In order to explain escalation, we needed all three concepts.

In addition, the conflict triangle needs to be complemented with the *existential* dimension of social conflict, since such conflicts often deal with issues of life and death: why am I exposed to this? Is there a meaning? Anyone that has met a survivor from life-threatening situations, knows how serious such issues can be, for that person. This means that we need to address both the "outside" and "inside" of a peace-building process, in order to—be likely to—achieve sustainability.

This is a transformation of Galtung's concept of "incompatibility" (of goals) into a need for a trustworthy treatment of goals, in practice what can be called "issue security." In the same way, the concept of "attitudes" in a spiraling process, needs to be transformed into a recognizing of one's "attitudes," that is one's identity, thus we use the concept of "identity security." Finally, the concept of behavior, meaning destruction of the counter-party's values, should be transformed into spatial security in all respects—no more fear, neither from people, nor from life conditions as a whole. In addition to these three concepts, we add "existential security," making the picture a complete argument for conditions for peaceful relations.

WHICH SECURITY?

Such a sustainable situation is then a state of "positive security" and even "positive peace." In Figure 5 the concept of "security" is used in this wide sense of the word, more or less as is used in "human security"—where it can be understood as "a stable provision of needs satisfaction." Also, since we stress the concept of "security" here, we can also make the observation, that from the history of the development of human rights, we could recognize this dimension as equal to President Roosevelt's "freedom from fear."

The four dimensions identified above relate to each other as in the figure below. *Existential security* is at hand when a society is ready to meet and respond to issues of this nature among its citizens. *Spatial security* provides physical security, both in terms of short-term safety and social order, "safety on the street," as well as long-term stability and trust in institutions responsible for law and order. Also the environmental dimensions of security—which also can be life-threatening—belong to this category. It is difficult to imagine a human space that is life-threatening (which is the issue this dimension deals with). All threats of that nature are spatial.

Figure 5. Four needs of security as a basis for peace-building

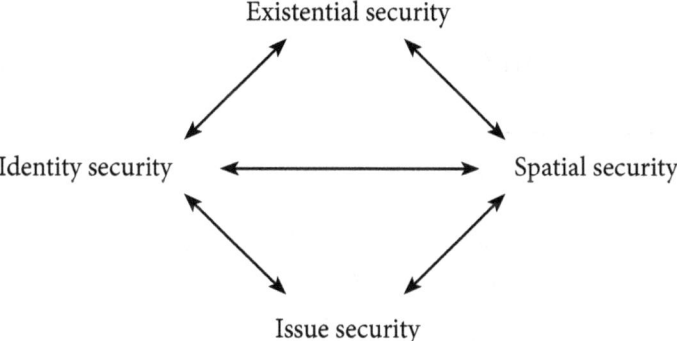

Identity security is the dimension for which many conflicts today are fought. Recognition and acknowledgement are important factors here, but also reconciliation with (former) enemies, irrespective of ethnicity or religion. Finally, *issue security* refers to the functioning and trust in institutions that manage and decide about concerns, of any nature basically, that citizens may bring up on the public, political arena—through parties, demonstrations, media, or other non-violent methods.

As the figure shows, there is a direct link between existential, identity, and spatial security, respectively, but not with issue security. This is so, since existential issues, empirically speaking, are empirically likely to refer to behavior (killing, destruction) and identity rather than to democratic or other institutions, as such. If this proves not to be true, we need a better figure!

There are "providers" of human rights, in the sense of principles and institutions, relevant for each of the four corners in the figure. If peace-building is a multidimensional process—which the figure implies—it would be interesting to identify some rights whose realization are likely to (contribute to) establish a peaceful relation between two of the concepts in the figure.

For instance, the right to freedom of expression, understood as a right to demonstrate peacefully, links the spatial and issue security corners to each other. Combining specific rights with the four corners and comparing real cases of peace-building—in a dyad approach or higher—would allow us to learn more about the linkage between Human Rights and Peace-Building. A more substantial description of possible contents is given in Table 5.

Table 5. Needs and providers of a peace structure

	Needs	Provider	Examples of a human rights basis
Existential security	Interpretation and understanding of fundamental life conditions	Philosophies; Religions; Belief systems	Universal Declaration of Human Rights
Identity security	Recognition; Education; Expression of identity	Legal protection; Schools; Multi-cultural society; Autonomy	Minority rights; Religious rights; Non-discrimination (group rights)
Spatial security	Territorial safety; Law and order; Environmental security	State system: central or decentralized	Convention against torture
Issue security	Expression of opinion; Mechanisms of political influence; Democracy	Media; Democratic education; Normative structures of pluralism	Rights of expression; Freedom of assembly; Freedom of movement

ANOTHER LINKAGE?

The single most important finding in social sciences regarding violence and political systems, is the observation that democracies don't fight each other.

The explanation for why it is in this way is however not a single one, but two major types of explanations exist. One is relying on the normative constraints that purportedly exists in democracies, i.e., citizens in democracies simply don't "want" to go to war, they believe other methods are possible in particular if the "enemy" is a democracy as well. The second explanation talks about internal, institutional constraints within democracies. This means that it is such a complicated decision-making process in a democracy to initiate war, that the idea falls apart through its own impracticality, so to speak.

From a human rights perspective it is even more interesting to follow the debate that emanates from this originally inter-state-based observation. Could it be, that also intra-state democratic conditions as well provide for (at least) less *internal* conflicts, than non-democratic conditions? With a conventional—election-oriented—definition of democracy, this seems not to be the case. Also (even strong) democracies deal violently with certain internal issues (India, Britain/Ireland, Spain, Turkey, etc.). Here, the issue of human rights comes in as an interesting contribution to what is generally a social science discussion. Maybe the realization of certain human rights—rather than a particular system of elections, such as "democracy"—could explain under what conditions peace can be maintained. Basically, the idea is, that the substance of many human rights variables in a context of this kind, might be as explanatory as many more structural (social science) variables. Here is a field open, for more in-depth studies and multi-disciplinary thinking.

Once again, the purpose is to describe, that through a conceptual approach to peace-building, one could test the explanatory value of human rights dimensions as contributors to peace-building.

An interesting position in this debate has also been developed by Michael Feher[3] who argues that a transitional process, from war to peace, is to be liked with a "civilizational jump." This implies, that justice before the "jump" is a different kind of justice, than after, and the same is the case with "reconciliation."

In a way, that is our observation, this view is mirroring the traditional view of (the need for) introducing and proclaiming war against an enemy—it means the introduction of the laws of war, without declaration of war, these laws were in principle not in force. Today's domination of civil wars, and gradual process of conflict, violence, and a prolonged armed conflict

3. Feher, "Terms of Reconciliation."

and wars has made this principle obsolete. But Feher can refer to it, as an argument for his view.

A useful overview of practices is the study of Iván Orozco Abad where he labels the dispute between the "doers of peace" and the "defenders of human rights" as a "family dispute."[4] Departing from the Latin American experience of dictatorships and self-imposed amnesties, Orozco brings up the convergence in Europe between human rights defenders and the peace movement during the last decade of the Iron Wall.

The Wall's existence led to the convergence of views and actions of the two groups in a way that illustrated the complementarity of peace/pacifism, and human rights, according to Orozco. However and later on, through the wars of Cambodia, former Yugoslavia, Rwanda, and elsewhere, the tension within the humanitarian family became all the more visible, in the end dividing the family into various groupings with different characteristics. Orozco identifies "politicians" vs. "lawyers" as representing conflict dimensions. Another one is between "pragmatics" and "purists," a third one between "the managers of conflict" and "the democratizers."[5]

Orozco argues for a balance between the two agendas, but ends his discussion in the midst of debating the Colombian situation, without really stating a final position on the "family dispute." A possible interpretation of Orozco can be made saying that a similar approach to the European experience of convergence between the peace and human rights movements could be developed in a generic way, i.e., as a way to overcome the striking injustices of Latin America—as was the Iron Wall.

Rodrigo Uprimny[6] identifies in a useful way the gradual shift that different cases of transition from "war to peace" illustrate—from the legacy of Nüremburg and similar cases of *imposed justice*, to cases of a strong reconciliatory approach to the dilemma of peace and justice. While also, according to Uprimny, Nüremburg and Bosnia represent *imposed justice*, Argentina and Chile are cases of *self-amnesty*, by the incumbent military governments. In Central America, on the other hand, it is possible to talk about *reciprocal pardons*, while South Africa, Uruguay, and Northern Ireland represent cases of *democratically legitimate* transitions, again according to Uprimny.

---

4. Orozco Abad, *Sobre los límites*.
5. Ibid.
6. Uprimny, *¿Justicia transicional sin transición?*

The scholarly literature on concepts such as "reconciliation" and "forgiveness" is obviously less developed than for human rights or international law, but a good exponent is Peter Digeser.[7] His book was published in the wake of the work of the South African TRC. It is probably fair to say, that archbishop Desmond Tutu has become the most well-known exponent for the view that reconciliation rather than punishment in periods of transition can be justified. One can say, that the South African TRC members developed a language of forgiveness and reconciliation directly linked to the concept of truth and confessions. Neither the South African lawyers, formulating the law that established the TRC and related legislation, nor Tutu or his fellow members of the South African TRC, are representing any simplistic view of neither punishment nor human rights. It was an "early"—that is early in the 1990s—process that came to have many followers later on. Maybe one could say, that the concept of "punishment" that was embraced in South Africa had a wider meaning in the immediate post-Apartheid context, than is usual in political and legal discourses elsewhere. The critical formula was to forgive but not forget.[8]

In such situations, three different arguments for the introduction of "reconciliation" as a political instrument, are found in the literature. The first argues that a country with a shattered legal, political, and economic system cannot give an over-riding priority to instituting a costly legal procedure that runs over decades, at the unavoidable expense of other sectors. Another view is that on the moral level there is a morass of responsibilities in all directions, making it in practice an impossible task to create justice in any reasonable sense of the word after, say, a decade-long civil war. A third view is that legal procedures are backward-looking, they focus on the past and past grievances—the least what is needed in a country that needs to plan for its future, and create visions of a joint future—friend and foe together.[9]

POWER AND GENDER DIMENSIONS

There is a big difference for any legal process—or peace process on the whole for that matter—if the parties have agreed to a result based on negotiation or a negotiated understanding (or an agreement) where *neither*

7. Digeser, *Political Forgiveness*. See also Shriver, *An Ethic for Enemies*.
8. Tutu, *No Future*.
9. For an overview of positions see Bell, *Peace Agreements*; Teitel, *Transitional Justice*.

RECONCILIATION AS POLITICS

side have been forced to give up militarily, on the one hand, and a situation where one of the sides can claim *military victory,* over the other. In the case of a victory of one side, it is not so that the loosing side does not have any bargaining power, but still, the situation is still fundamentally different from a negotiated one.

The language of reconciliation, irrespective of it being used at a political or inter-personal level, is by some regarded as "soft," as an expression of weakness, thus often something women, or children or otherwise weak persons in general, are likely to be more prone of, than other groups. Some critics would claim that accepting reconciliation on a social or political level is basically a view of the Other that risks becoming deceptive, in practice a meek and self-denying attitude. While it is not uncommon that groups that have committed serious crimes in the name of *machismo*, masculinity, and power—such as for instance the Colombian paramilitary leaders—are among the first to accept possibilities of (degrees of) reconciliation. Their switch from one language to another is an obvious political survival strategy, and can be seen as co-opting the concept.

Close to the gender dimension lies the concept of "victim." It makes more profound the gender analysis by accepting also the theoretical possibility of making in one sense powerful individuals "victims" in another sense. While "victimhood" defines a person's status in relation to a particular conflict—(s)he can be victim, perpetrator and/or both—and thus expresses different levels of access to power at various moments in time, the gender dimension stresses the long-term roles of the same individuals. Both concepts—gender and victim, respectively—and their relationship, with changing gender roles as a possible consequence, needs therefore to be part of the analysis of reconciliation processes.

RECONCILIATION OR FORGIVENESS?

As an early and general reflection on the relationship between politics and reconciliation, an observation can be that reconciliation is not a "political process" of traditional type; it is rather a "pre-political" process in the sense that it is a de facto recognition that "politics" in its essence, up till that point, has failed to produce an acceptable social situation (=war), and that in order to avoid something even worse, one or another form of "reconciliation" is necessary. By nature, reconciliation is not a totally individual process—as can be forgiveness. There has to be at least two individuals that can reconcile with each other. In this sense, reconciliation is a *relational* concept. Reconciliation is thus providing a tool for building relationships. It is, to use sociological language, a *structural* concept, which for that particular reason can serve in a political context, and not only in a private or individual setting.

It is this structural, relation building capacity of "reconciliation" which makes it relevant and useful in a political discourse and practice. The latter is however not the case for "forgiveness." Forgiveness is—or can be—a one-sided act that can be expressed without any reciprocal action from the intended recipient's side. In practice there can very well be cases of mutual forgiveness, but the concept as such does not require this to happen, in order to be meaningful. As a consequence, forgiveness, when used in a political vocabulary, can at worst function as a kind of imposition on individuals, something that goes against the democratic nature of the whole process.[10]

Reconciliation, in order to be a useful concept, also has to relate to the content, the nature of the relationship. I would argue, that it is too weak, to equal reconciliation with "being nice." This would place the concept among fundamental rules for social interaction. There has to be some more to it. In sum, reconciliation cannot be forgiveness, and cannot be just to be friendly.

THE RELATIONAL COMPONENT

A legal process does not normally involve any form of message or interaction between victim and perpetrator. In court proceedings the two sides try to convince the court, not each other. As noted above, in a reconciliation process it is "the other side"—being it a victim or a perpetrator—that primarily addresses each other, not, for instance, a commission for truth and reconciliation. A major purpose of reconciliation is however to influence relations, not necessarily on a personal level, but on the level where it was before the injustices etc. started. The assumption, then, is that the moral balance in a society is probably best restored on the level where it was broken. Without this relational component, again, it is hard to call a process of reconciliation; it would be counter-intuitive to the general understanding of the concept.

---

10. See Shriver, *An Ethic for Enemies*; Digeser, *Political Forgiveness*.

RECONCILIATION AS POLITICS

MORAL AND LEGAL CLAIMS

There is an ethical dimension as well, in "reconciliation," which makes it representative for the message that individuals and others would like to send when they reconcile. The fundamental message is, that an individual, a group, or even a country is prepared to overlook, at least to some degree, legitimate claims (moral, legal, material) against the other person/side, for the sake of re-establishing relations based on the perpetrator's acknowledgement of the victim's suffering and a responsibility in this connection. The various components mentioned above, making up a "reconciliation process"—such as acknowledgement, contrition, truth telling, reparation, and justice—are all instruments for this. Reconciliation processes, with their different mechanisms, deal with a situation that a society's regular institutions are not built for, and therefore not able, to deal with effectively, neither legally, socially, nor ethically.

Reconciliation in a Legal Framework

In the introduction the question was asked how it could be that "reconciliation" made its way into the political discourse and language at all. The literature in the subject tends either to deal with the justice dimension, the socio-psychological dimension or the forgiveness/remorse dimension. The above stated assumption for the discussion here is that reconciliation has a component that includes the re-establishment of broken relations. A legal approach to these situations has been developed through the concept of *transitional justice*, which is a temporary legal order that besides its ability to try violations in court(s), often includes systems of reparation, truth telling and reform of the security sector as parts of a package for institutional reforms. Its relation to reconciliation is a matter of debate in itself, and is not in focus of this study; however, it is part of the political and conceptual context of reconciliation.[11]

The Question of Impunity or Amnesty

The question of amnesty—and impunity as well—lies in the tension between the morally unique position that a state as well as a victim has to be able to grant. The individual can forgive on the moral level, the state

---

11. Teitel, *Transitional Justice*, is still a standard work.

can give amnesty on the legal level. What is important for the state, and also for an individual, is that this act is connected to something special: a unique event, a situation no one could foresee (in legislation or in real life), it shall not be repeated, and the like. Our normal understanding of law, as something that should be applied in an equal way, is undermined by a praxis of amnesty, and therefore amnesty is often not based on legal grounds but on grounds that other institutions handle in a society, such as a presidency. Likewise, most likely will a person, that constantly forgives his or her friends and foes for whatever they do, be regarded with some skepticism. We expect the forgiver to be restrained in that practice.

We need in this context also to note, that there is a risk that state leaders, from an economic or populist perspective and dealing with a weak police and court system, including prisons, are likely to consider reduced punishment, or even amnesty, as a way of dealing with weaknesses. This is easy to criticize from a legal point of view, but the interesting question is what will happen if this weakness is disregarded, and things are set to move on *as if* the situation was "normal." That will as well cause violations of some human rights, most certainly.[12] We are here touching on an aspect of the classical dilemma of peace versus justice.

The Reconciliation Debate

It seems that from the vast debate over issues of reconciliation, and subsequent demands and debates over compensation, reparation, restoration, pardon, acknowledgment, and recognition, that two main issues penetrate the whole discussion. As of now, I think it is possible to integrate all cases of debate issues in this particular formula, described in Table 6 below. After further studies it might be possible, and very interesting I am sure, to draw more complex conclusions about their relationship.

It takes its point of departure in the moral complexity of a situation, and the extent to which a society or a state is able to manage—legally, socially etc.—its own crimes/processes, etc. A "morally complex" situation is a situation where both/all sides in a conflict have committed serious crimes/violations of human rights against each other, often over a long period of time. A "state's ability" refers to the material, institutional, and political capacity of a state to undertake systematic and fair prosecutions

---

12. These themes are developed in Abu-Nimer, *Reconciliation*; Humphrey, *Politics of Atrocity*.

and/or rectifications of committed crimes/violations, given its resources and development needs and prospects. Here we deal with OECD countries, as well as the poorest 25 in the world. Situations of "reconciliation debates" are found "everywhere." Thus the examples are quite diversified, however, in common they have the introduction of "reconciliation" as a politically valid concept, and relevant for a given situation under debate.

Table 6. Reconciliation debates on state/community level—examples of issues

	High ability of states/ communities to deal with violations	Limited ability of states/ communities to deal with violations
High moral complexity of the situation	Global management of historical discrimination	Internal conflict processes in Colombia, Sri Lanka, Kenya, Philippines
Low moral complexity of the situation	Current, ongoing discrimination of indigenous groups, ethnic and religious minorities	South Africa Apartheid liberation process; East Timor independence process; Uganda and LRA indictments

The most visible debate today is held in square 4. While South Africa and Timor Leste have chosen a path that used reconciliation commissions—for reasons of avoiding continued internal conflict/war—Uganda has withdrawn its initial support to the ICC for issuing an arrest order of five Lord's Resistance Army (LRA) top leaders, claiming it interrupts a possible peace process. In all these situations, the moral complexity of the situation is low—the perpetrators are well known, largely one-sided and their general (not personal) responsibility is questioned neither nationally nor internationally.

Square 1 is in a way "the opposite." It deals with our (generation's) responsibility for historic wrongdoings of previous generations. This debate touches as well on the responsibility of anthropology to contribute to return of objects, as it relates to how to deal with historic monuments, and—more important—to what extent, if any, has a living generation a responsibility for wrongdoings by its predecessors?[13]

The two other squares do not need any further comment here. They illustrate two other well-known cases. The point with Table 6 is to identify dimensions that seem to bring a structure to the phenomenon of "reconciliation" in a political context. This is still an emerging debate, and approached from a variety of positions.

---

13. Thompson, *Taking Responsibility*, is an excellent overview of the issues raised in these debates, referring to the Australian case of Aboriginal population and Australia.

6

Political Reconciliation and Human Rights—Matching or Not?

"Human rights" is a concept that is widely known and part of an established vocabulary in many societies, even if the knowledge about its real content may not be on the same level. When it comes to the concept of "reconciliation" and in particular "political reconciliation," the case may be the opposite: many have a personal experience of reconciling—with other persons, with themselves, or with "fate"—but the concept has appeared comparatively recently in the political arena.

For the purpose here, there is definitively an interesting link between the two concepts, since they originate from the same family of dignity-based values. It is not without reason that, as we have observed already in previous chapters, psychologists, psychotherapists, and theologians have made use of the concept—they are thereby illustrating the basis of reconciliation in human dignity.

While human rights can be viewed as an operationalization of human dignity, the point of departure taken here is that reconciliation can be viewed as a restoration of human dignity in human relations. But is this where similarity stops? Human rights are formalized in international documents and applied in legal processes and national legislation. Reconciliation is, on the other hand, a process between individuals and groups, and even if it may end in a formalized document or an agreement of some sort, the concept gets its content very much by those who apply it in a given moment. Universality is at best searched for in the *method of reconciling*, rather than in a specific outcome of that process. For human rights it is rather the opposite: irrespective of method, the outcome should be equal and applied in a symmetric way.

The question is then if these two concepts, and the perspectives they represent can be working against each other, could they even be competing approaches in a political context? Or is there a potential for them to complement each other as strategies for conflict resolution and peace?

A VIEW OF DIGNITY

Human dignity can be regarded as a constitutive quality of the human being (as opposed to an acquired). A quality that is formative for the human being from the first day, and where human development throughout life is *not* a prerequisite for dignity, but a way of expressing, experiencing, and promoting it. Throughout life, therefore, the human beings experience their own dignity, in different ways and in different contexts, and at the same time observe—and hopefully respect—the dignity of others. Human dignity is something that can be experienced not only as respectful relations, or during "a relaxed and casual afternoon with friends," but also—and sometimes more so—under mistreatment and violations of one's person. Actually, it is probably correct to say "without dignity no violation." Unfortunately and very tragically, many persons experience their dignity only when violated.

Experiencing Dignity?

Can we identify typical situations for when human dignity is experienced? The Table 7 indicates that there is both a social and individual aspect of such situations, as well as a subjective and an objective.

The right to life, freedom, and personal security are often mentioned as fundamental dimensions of human rights. This is true, while at the same time, there is no basis for putting one right before the other on the level of principle. If we accept, that human rights is an interpretation and operationalization of human dignity, we can look at reconciliation in a political context as the restoration of human dignity that has been violated in political conflict.

Political reconciliation means in practice often a reassessment of a specific history or situation in a direction of mutuality and respect. In this way it comes close to expressing human dignity.

On the collective level, dignity is expressed both subjectively ("We the peoples," from the UN Charter) and objectively, that is from an actor perspective which is based on a common feeling of being dignified and therefore having the (moral) right to act as a unit. The expression of this objectively identified dignity is then, of course, human rights, expressed in so many different ways, but the Universal Declaration is a good example, maybe still the best.

Table 7. Experiences identifying human dignity

	Subjective type	Objective type
Collective social level	"We the peoples"; Civil society	The UN Charter Universal Declaration of Human Rights
Individual level	Religious, philosophical experiences; Meditation, mysticism	The constitution of the individual human being; The wealth of the universe including the Creation

The individual person has not only a collective but of course also a personal basis for dignity. Without even using or knowing the concept, the dignity of a person is a relational quality expressed and experienced in religious and/or philosophical contexts, but as well in daily relation-building with other persons. The dignity we know of is the one shown by others, the one reflected upon by ourselves, and the one shared by others through a multitude of communications over time and space, from caves to social media.

Human rights is a concept with several decades of use, among broad community concepts. However, its meaning and consequences may not be as great as one may think after such a long period, neither in a given country nor globally. The concept of reconciliation is in some ways in the opposite situation: many have personal experience of reconciliation but the concept has only recently taken place in a broader public political discourse.

In the West, the dominating Christian tradition has for hundreds of years had the idea of reconciliation at the heart of its teachings and traditions. Linguistically this has sometimes taken on a more punitive character (such as in the German and Scandinavian languages) than in Latin languages as well as in English. Many in a modern and secular society believe today that the concept of reconciliation has nothing of value to bring to a (secular) political discussion, claiming the view that it only makes less clear any political analysis when, or if, it brings in religious or spiritual aspects.

One can, as an almost spontaneous first reflection, reflect on whether it makes sense to bring together such seemingly diametrically opposed concepts such as human rights and reconciliation, or not. Certainly, they have a common normative basis in that they formulate the expression of human dignity. But practically thinking, they represent two very different approaches to achieve this.

SOME POINTS OF COMPARISON

Initially, some fundamental differences between human rights and reconciliation were identified. Let's go systematically through some aspects of difference.

Unilateral Concern or a Mutual Act?

Human rights are a unilateral concern, foremost for states—reconciliation is a mutual act, foremost among individuals. Doesn't this indicate a gulf between human rights and political reconciliation? Human rights should be defended by the state and when it is not able or willing to do that, we can as citizens claim our right against the state, not on the basis of capacity or heritage or class, but on the basis of our rights as humans. This is a very asymmetric relationship—it doesn't matter how big a state, or how young a person. The rights are there. Reconciliation, on its part, is a very different thing: it can never be claimed, possibly asked for, but not enforced or imposed.

But this is a superficial observation. Human rights will be realized, as a deliberate policy, only in communities where the human being is a subject, an active and politically significant actor. And reconciliation will be realized as a deliberate act only between people who respect each other's experiences, "stories," and by virtue of this want to make it to be to the benefit of all. In the process that every political decision in a democracy is rooted, we find the same dimensions of reciprocity and respect for truth and justice, which is a must for reconciliation processes. This also means that we reach a point where we must consider also the state as a morally responsible actor. We may consider the state as morally responsible if human rights are not defended, for instance.

This implies, logically, that if the state is morally liable, then the state is seen as a moral actor, which also means that the state may, for example, forgive when something wrong is committed against the state. If the state then represents what is held in common in a society, then obviously the common can be seriously injured in certain situations. Any civil war can testify to this.

This means also that when many have suffered from harm, one can also imagine that the state expresses demands on behalf of them, demands for compensation. But it may also be times when the state, for the common good ("the national interest"), refrains from claiming what it could claim, of a variety of reasons, of course, and in a settlement based on mutual recognition prefer to establish new relationships between political actors before making all the claims morally possible.

In the practical work with human rights and political reconciliation, the similarities between the two appear greater than what a strictly conceptual reflection may suggest. For instance, the many truth and reconciliation commissions around the world have brought up the question, in almost every country in which they were created, if it is possible to establish a policy of national reconciliation, for example, after civil war. If so, what would characterize such a policy?

Reconciliation is allegedly often the goal of a national peace process. An element of reconciliation should reasonably be an element in the process, and the possible examples of this are many: dialogues, symbolic manifestations, individual discussions, workshops, collection of individual stories, public hearings, open conversations about everyday threats and problems. What is important is, in fact, to avoid the political overtones to create specific public situations which suggest that "now we are reconciled." However, it is quite possible that later, after a number of actions / processes with broad participation, political or religious leader may say that "we have achieved a level of reconciliation during recent years" or something similar.

The question "when are we reconciled?" needs however further reflection. Any peace process, for example, has its violated rights to restore. The point here is that in a process of many different activities, human rights are gradually defended as well. When this happens, the foundation for reconciliation is laid down. Again—it is on the practical level that human rights and reconciliation processes can be brought together in a useful and interesting way, in spite of the contrasting formulation above!

Human Rights Is a Substance Category—Reconciliation Is a Process Concept

The use of the concept of reconciliation, in political processes, has come to be dominated by national peace processes after civil war (as in Sierra Leone, Guatemala, and East Timor) or system changes after dictatorships or Apartheid (as in Chile, Argentina, and South Africa). In direct connection to the use of the concept of reconciliation in a political context a few major moral and political problems present themselves: does political reconciliation on the national level require legal justice first—or should reconciliation come first and formal justice be held later? It is a simplified question, but it is at the same time very real in many countries as they face a total collapse in their legal or administrative systems, but somehow have managed to control violence and look forward to restart their state-building project. Somehow, there is a relation-building component that is lost, if the two approaches are contrasted against each other: justice first, or reconciliation first?

When human rights are realized, it means for instance that people's living conditions are decent and fair. Some rights are strictly individual, others relate directly to a communities' lives and interests, such as education, health, and the right to assembly. (And we still have not talked about group rights here.) There is a strong relationship-building component of the application of human rights, not least in the rights that provide basic capabilities to create a democratic society.

The central moments of relation-building are now in focus. Nor at this point is there a necessary compartmentalization between our two concepts—since a process without content is meaningless.

Human Rights Is a "Right"—Reconciliation Is a "Gift"

What can be demanded and what can be given, between persons? If human rights is precisely that, meaning something that is agreed between people(s) on the basis of a common understanding of human dignity, and if at the same time these rights cannot be met, they should be possible to claim—on good grounds.

RECONCILIATION AS POLITICS

Reconciliation must be a voluntary, mutual and independent process. In practice, reconciliation—political or not—is an exchange of a (social) gift between two or more parties. This exchange represents a new capability, a new resource given to each other. Let us develop this as shown in Table 8.

Table 8. Human dignity as a right and a gift

	Human dignity as a right	*Human dignity as a gift*
One-sided relation to the Other	The individual person can claim the right from the state (the opposite is not possible)	Forgiveness; Personal gifts; "Luck in life"
Two-sided relation to the Other	Mutual rights are made into a mix of rights and duties, i. e., citizenship	Reconciliation; Two-way relation of giving (not of taking)

SOME PRINCIPLE POINTS OF DEPARTURE

The formulation of a foundational moral basis for political reconciliation will have to rest on some key principles. In the following we will draw from the reflections above in this chapter, and link them to some formulations of principle in order to see what such a basis would look like.

The Victim—Always the First Concern

Victims suffer from many things, but one of them besides all other aspects is the need to be recognized—not as a victim by concept or identity, necessarily, but as someone that has suffered from a harmful experience and therefore has been exposed to threats to one's existence. To have this experienced recognized, listened to and not rejected or silenced to the extent the individual person would like to have it, should be a driving duty and concern for any serious process towards political reconciliation. Such experiences are both individual and social, they are sometimes shared by people in great numbers, and may bring strong political messages from that. What is true is, that the situation, in all its complexity, is different from the past—polarized maybe but different. Any process starting from such a point of departure needs to have the victim's perspective as its first concern.

That raises of course the question about who is, in the end, a victim? The discussion is well-known: "victim one day, perpetrator the next" or "perpetrator as army soldier, but victim as enrolled soldier-father without alternatives in life" and similar expressions put the finger on the complexity. Generalizations about individuals or groups are not of good help.

Truth—The Driving Motive

It is hard to imagine a process of reconciliation, or compensation or justice, which is not based on a serious investigation of what did happen, where and when? Truth has two roles to play here: it sorts out what happened, but it also establishes a platform, a basis for talking about the future. The new knowledge that is created through a truth process will be part of court processes, history books, personal memories, and in conversations for a long time about the common history of those living in a region or a country.

There is also another effect of truth establishment, and that is that there is no—or less— room for (all the) lies and rumors that until now have taken the space of imagination, hopes, and "plausible facts" that always emerge from conversations about the uncertain. Some of these hypotheses served as possible softeners of a threatening and hard future—should the alternative be the truth. Truth may make people free, but also suffer and exposed to a new reality, where the hope has to take another form, find another basis.

Change—A Necessary Precondition

The political reconciliation is a process, a political process. Actually, the point of having reconciliation is "change," and it would not be "reconciliation" unless there was a clear and indispensable movement of attitude and action among those involved. Since polarization is a fundamental feature in social conflict, political reconciliation contains actions which are "negative" in the sense of withdrawal, reduction of tension, de-polarizing expressions in public and the like. The absence of demands that were there before, the use of a more open and less confrontational language are signals of change from a level of confrontation that needed polarization to be sustained.

RECONCILIATION AS POLITICS
Creation as a Realistic Possibility

Some of the claims that are made by parties or other actors in conflict resolution processes express a concern that it is not possible to foresee, or even "control," the consequences of a certain initiative, and therefore it should not be taken. In response to such a view, it must be a principle in the application of political reconciliation that to the extent the process is serious, it is also most likely to create both a positive outcome on the basis of what is controlled, and a positive outcome through the release of capacities and other resources that otherwise were demanded by the polarization preceding the process. There is always a level of uncertainty in political life, and until the opposite is proved, there has to be a principle of positive appreciation when actors actively reject an old pattern of relations and embark on new ones.

The idea of human rights is rather to prevent and protect, than repair and restore. But since we—as human beings—are not capable of building societies, on the basis of common and agreed principles, that meet not even the most fundamental human needs, we need a system of human rights as a corrective to this inability. The rights have to be there as a claim for dignity. It is a vertical relation only that can try to do something about it, since the horizontal relations between all human beings were not able.

The perspective of reconciliation—political or not—is a horizontal process as much as a rights-perspective is vertical. The purpose of political reconciliation is to create moral symmetry, for victims as well as for perpetrators and irrespective of levels of society.

From this way of describing the relationship between the two concepts, one can argue that the two are complementary and actually also necessary for building a society of human dignity. Human rights is there to compensate for the weakness of humanity, and the violations of rights that come from that, and political reconciliation is there to restore our relations, when these rights have been violated.

7

Legal Frameworks and International Peace

When the United Nations was formed in 1945, the state was the founding and unquestioned unit of international order. When the Secretary-General of the United Nations in 1992, Boutros Boutros-Ghali, describes the international situation, and the conditions for the work of the UN after the end of the Cold War, he finds it necessary to note, that when it comes to the United Nations "The foundation-stone... is and must remain the State. Respect for its fundamental sovereignty and integrity are crucial to any common international progress."[1] The reasoning behind this statement was, what he and many saw at the time, namely that the state as an idea and ideal, and as a solution of the needs and interests of "we the peoples," gradually had been questioned—a development that actually had started already when the United Nations Organization was created. The United Nations was institutionalized while two international processes took place at the same time: the Cold War, and the period of de-colonization. The latter was a time when many new states were created, a process the UN itself was highly instrumental in through its mechanisms for de-colonization. It is one of the United Nations' greatest achievements—although forgotten by many today—to administrate a peaceful process towards independence of a large number of states, particularly, on the African continent.

The state—as an ideal and structure for peace and development for peoples around the world—turned however not sufficiently out, as a provider of rights and space for large groups of people, and it became challenged in the way it had constructed itself out. The formation process of the

---

1. United Nations, *An Agenda for Peace*.

new states did not necessarily correspond to the needs and interests of the populations in their territories, so many peoples who did not get a territory for state-building, initiated armed rebellions of different force and durability. This development came to question states and their constitutional designs, something which the Secretary-General rightly foresaw as an increasing problem for the UN and for the whole international community of states and organizations. The period from the early 1990s up till today is only a broad confirmation of that development.

At the same time, the state was, and is, challenged from another direction: the internationalization of relations and the globalization of economies and idea generation that it brings. The state's monopoly and control of its economic basis is diminishing due to this development, and its ability to control the generation and flow of ideas is reduced as well, something particularly worrying for those states whose power groups are basing their position on this particular control.

Having realized this, Boutros-Ghali added that even if the state is the UN foundation-stone, its exclusive sovereignty was never matched by reality. The reality that has been there has instead been a constant challenge to the established states' perception of themselves as legitimate holders of sovereignty. What everyone knew was of course, that a "state" can create a certain level of sovereignty without the acceptance or explicit recognition of other states as being a "state."[2]

Another step along the same development was taken through the introduction of the concept of Responsibility to Protect, which was accepted by the UN General Assembly in 2005. It is built on the idea that if sovereignty is given by states to other states, and therefore the same states can take back this recognition, under certain conditions. The most important one is, that if a state leader fails to defend the rights of the population (which most often in practice means the leader is the violator of the population's rights), this is a basis for a series of initiatives according to the principle of Responsibility to Protect. Libya in 2011, and its leader at the time Mohammad Khadaffi, was the first country to be targeted by the UN under this new principle. Later on, many believed that the Syrian conflict also met the criteria for an intervention similar to the Libyan.

---

2. It is not the attempt of the terrorist organization Daesh, to label itself an "Islamic State," that is the most serious challenge to the state as a founding unit of international peace and security, but rather the many movements of local autonomy or secession which often they become armed.

How come that Boutros-Ghali at all found it necessary to make an observation that from a UN point of view would be regarded as self-evident? The world had changed, it is true, from one where wars between states were rare—and suppressed by the Cold War—and where civil wars were controlled by the two super-powers in that war. In 1992, then, this was no longer the case—the control was no longer there, with the dissolution of the Soviet Union and a subsequent changing policy from the United States. Instead, 1991 became the most violent—in terms of number of armed conflicts—since the end of the Second World War with 51 ongoing armed conflicts that year.[3]

For the international legal system, for international humanitarian law as well as for international human rights law, the weakening of the state is a problem of principle and practice. The states are the signatories of international humanitarian law conventions, and primary duty-bearers in the human rights system. But for human rights this is a problem: weakening of the state means weakening of units with legally binding obligations in the international system.

PEACE AGREEMENTS

The classical view from history of the peace agreement as an inter-state document of highest level and unquestionable content is today, although still a formal agreement, by many signatories formed as a process document, guiding steps of ending of violence, a long-term process of national dialogue and reconstruction and a final implementation of a new order, including processes of memory and, at best, even reconciliation.

Obviously, the formal peace agreement is the foundation stone in a peace process. Interstate peace agreements are regulated by the Vienna Convention from 1969 while intrastate agreements, for instance between a government and a guerilla movement or political party, are in principle an internal political affair. Since almost all armed conflicts and wars are internal, this increases the necessity to base the agreement in a politically negotiated context. This means that some attempts at getting an end to violence and destruction are made rather "early," that is, under circumstances where the political will to end the conflict are not clearly expressed. Also, different types of initiatives, from other states as well as from the civil society in an affected state, are often taken, sometimes to the benefit for the process as

3. Pettersson and Wallensteen, "Armed Conflict."

a whole, sometimes they are only a way for the parties to find a fig-leaf for regrouping and maintain influence.

The status of an agreement affects directly the political cost of breaking it. Some cease-fire agreements in civil wars are broken as soon as the signatures are written, clearly because the process of developing an agreement was the important thing, not its result. In other cases the parties knew that serious violations of an agreement would have significant political costs and therefore withheld actions which in the end would have hurt their interests. The inclusion of high-level witnesses, political and/or religious, increases the solemn nature of the signing and give weight to documents that in themselves may still be disputed and criticized, when signed.

These observations lead us up to a major dilemma of peace processes: "justice first, and then reconciliation, or reconciliation first, and then justice."

Moral Dilemmas in Peace Processes

Each legal order is confronted with moral dilemmas in the wake of a peace process after internal armed conflict—as long as it cares about the conflict's history at all. José Zalaquett summarized some dilemmas already in 1995 in the wake experiences in connection to the Chilean Truth Commission, one of the models for later commissions including the South African. Zalaquett has identified a number of issues which the Chilean process had to wrestle with:

- if there is a cease-fire and elections are to be held—should leaders of armed groups be allowed to be elected while they still hold arms in their organizations?
- should demobilized soldiers be integrated in a swift process, meaning their violations may never be brought to the surface again, or should they first be tried—something that takes time and can lead to recurring armed conflict?
- shall constitutions be written and introduced as part of a peace process, rather than as part of a regular constitutional process in a parliament?

- shall refugees be allowed a quick return even if new families have settled in their former houses and a return would cause immediate and daily conflicts?[4]

Dilemmas of this kind are here to illustrate the moral environment in which also concepts of reconciliation, conflict resolution, and state-building are discussed. These dilemmas are maybe dilemmas in a particular moral sphere, constituted by a modern state with democratic ideals. However, what is at hand is a set of triangular relations between different systems or "spheres of justice," so to say. They all have a role to play in the aftermath of armed conflicts, and they can be described as in the Figure 6.

Figure 6. Three types of legal systems and their relations

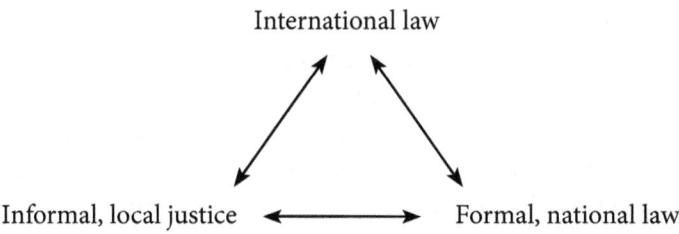

The traditional, national legal system is always the natural point of reference when legal matters arise, but in the aftermath of civil wars this system may be shattered and dysfunctional, something which opens space both for the local, informal and traditional normative systems that still play important roles in many societies. However, the international community may as well agree on setting up a special panel, a tribunal, in the country concerned, and apply international legal instruments that are applicable for the situation.

At worst, to put it that way, there could be three different legal systems that claim legitimacy and capacity to deal with perpetrators as well as victim's claims, in the wake of an internal armed conflict. This is of course not in any way a good situation. While the relation between the national and international levels depend on formal agreements there is normally no such arrangement within states, even if many states try to regulate legal systems between various groups, including ethnic and religious groups. Finally, the

4. Zalaquett, "Confronting Human Rights."

greatest distance is likely to appear between the international level and the local, traditional level. While principles should not necessarily have to be "opposed" or deviating from each other, the language, motivations and cases they are based upon are likely to differ and therefore also the essence of the legal principles are likely to be different. Again, these three legal orders, or systems, are relevant for dealing with harm that is done during armed conflict, or during an authoritarian regime/military regime or dictatorship.

As Figure 6 illustrates, there is a challenge for everyone interested in establishing a normative basis, a fundamental platform for normative reasoning, with global legitimacy. Is that possible at all, and is it something worth striving for? While there are different positions on this matter, it should be said, however, that as long as we propone human rights on a universal level, as responsibilities for the state vis-à-vis the individual person, it is hard to see how universality as a principle for normative development could be rejected.

The impression is sometimes that reconciliation is an extension of the work and spirit of transitional justice but for times and cases beyond its reach, it is supposed to be effective in the minds and moral landscapes of men and women who have to live with injustices of the past where no more recognition from the society of their suffering can be expected.

8

From East Timor to Timor Leste

The concepts and characteristics of a political reconciliation process discussed in the previous chapters, were to a good extent illustrated by the political transformation that East Timor went through during the 1990s and the first decade of the third millennium. This is so not only because East Timor was a major UN operation at the time, actually the largest, but also because it contained a number of policies and practices that relate to the concept of political reconciliation—from the political leadership's principles of reconciliation based on cultural traditions and strategic considerations.

An institutional expression of these principles was the establishment of a Commission for Reception, Truth and Reconciliation (CAVR). Another one is based on a policy of friendly relations that Timor Leste has developed with the former occupying power, Indonesia, something which included a bi-lateral Commission of Truth and Friendship (CTF) between the two states, Timor Leste and Indonesia. The transformation of identity, that this small territory underwent in this period, is illustrated in this text, where the name East Timor is used with reference to the period up to independence in 2002, and when referring to the period thereafter, the new republic's name is more appropriate, Timor Leste.[1]

In this chapter, and the following, we will use East Timor/Timor Leste as an example and point of reference for some of the earlier discussed aspects of political reconciliation.

---

1. The full name of the new state is The Democratic Republic of Timor Leste.

RECONCILIATION AS POLITICS

Already in the first chapter, in Table 1, we noted that peace processes of today often include a large variety of components. These components have different movers, purposes, and mandates but are all supposed to contribute to a regulation of issues that are created by the nature of armed conflicts of today—the civil war, and its characteristics of impacting not only on defense forces and irregular armies and fighters, but to varying degrees also upon the civil population, on its daily life as well as its prospects for the future.

The dissolution of the political and military struggle inside and outside of East Timor, in the late 1990s and the first years of the new millennium, contains examples of many elements of such a comprehensive peace process. But before that could happen, an intricate series of events ended the operation of one of the last colonial territories in the world.

EVERYTHING HAS A HISTORY

The island north of Australia called Timor was already five hundred years ago exposed to Portuguese colonial interest. As time went by, the Portuguese established presence in the island, not least with the help of missionaries and traders, and gradually agreed with relevant authorities of what now is Indonesia and the colonizing states of those areas, about a borderline between the Eastern and Western parts of Timor.

The Portuguese tradesmen that arrived in the 1500s, landed in the northern parts of East Timor, in an area which also today belongs to Timor Leste but in the form of an exclave—an area outside the main territory of a state—called Oecussi. This area is located within the Indonesian part of the island Timor, West Timor.[2] Its status as such has never been challenged in the recent conflict. East Timor was one of the most distant Portuguese colonial outposts, useful for what it was worth to have an area where ships and bring in fresh staple food in South East Asian waters, bordering to the Pacific.[3]

Even if the Portuguese were not the first outsiders to create a foothold on the island of Timor, the Portuguese arrival became lasting over time.

---

2. A final border line for Oecussi was not established until 1916.

3. Other Portuguese posts of comparable size were Macao on mainland China, having today a somewhat similar arrangement as Hong Kong. A similar case is Goa, on the Indian West coast. Goa was overtaken by India in the 1960s without larger protests from Portugal, which at the time had a military government.

The sandalwood of Timor attracted tradesmen in South East Asia already from the early days. Sandalwood was however overtaken as the main trading commodity in the nineteenth century by other goods, such as coffee, potatoes, sugar cane, and wheat.[4]

Turning to the past century, East Timor became a battle-ground during the Second World War. For the Japanese army, on its way to Australia, it was a strategic piece of land. After the war, the republic of Indonesia was formed on the basis of the Dutch colonial territories in the region, territories of which East Timor was not a part. Thus Portugal continued as a colonial power ruling in East Timor after the Second World War. It was not until 1974–1975 that the military regime in Portugal at the time had to give up its control of state power, and, subsequently, a de-colonization process was initiated among Portuguese holdings around the world, by the new and democratic Portuguese government. Thus several Portuguese holdings became independent in the following years—with the exception of East Timor, however.

The combination of regional trade, European colonialism, relatively disinterested regional powers, and strong local traditions, not the least linguistically, has created a fascinating mix in the East Timorese society. While the total population in 1975 was estimated to 680,000, 97 percent of them were East Timorese. (Today the figure is over one million.) The remaining parts were mainly Chinese businessmen with families, a few thousands, a small Arab community, Portuguese of recent origin, some of which were deported outside the country by the military regimes in Portugal (*deportados*), and Indonesians.[5] The East Timorese count their lines of origin in two directions—the Vedo-Australians and the Melanesians, the latter sharing the same history as the inhabitants of Papua New-Guinea. As in this country there is also in East Timor a wide variety of local languages, where some have certain coverage, such as Makassae, Mambai, and Kemac, respectively, with a few hundred thousand users, while many others are small and regionally very concentrated. *Tetum* is the most widely spoken local language, and it is today, in the independent Timor Leste, a national language, besides Portuguese, the official language.

James Dunn gives an account of how surprised he was on his first visit to East Timor, in 1962, when saying, "I was struck by the racial mix at every level of government. The chief justice was Goan and his wife Chinese, the

4. Dunn, *East Timor*, 16.
5. Ibid., chapter 1.

leading surgeon African and the director of customs Timorese."[6] Portugal was the power-holder, but it was weak and dependent on Chinese businessmen for the trade and on local people for administration as well as for maintaining an army. Portugal's presence was never larger than a few thousands, European soldiers included, and for long periods it was an even much smaller contingent.

Although far away from Lisbon, the fate of a colony is nevertheless shaped from its distant capital. East Timor was not a critical geographical area for Portugal, by no means comparable to Mozambique, Angola, or Guinea-Bissau. Not even to Goa or Macao. From a development point of view, basic modern infrastructure remained in Dili an unknown reality longer than for most comparable cities. Portugal did not invest in the modernization of East Timor—a fact that Indonesia thought should help integrate East Timor with Indonesia.

Portugal could not withstand the developments in Asia, whenever they impacted on East Timor. During the Second World War, for instance, Australia, in particular, felt that the Japanese might use East Timor as a base. Therefore, as a preventive measure, the Allied forces occupied the island only ten days after the Japanese attack on Pearl Harbor. Japan was pushing south, towards Australia at the time, then attacked East Timor and pushed the Allied out of the island in 1943. Japan stayed on there, till the end of the war.

One can say, that Portugal hold on to East Timor by default—since Portugal got a foothold on the island during its period of expansion on the seas, why not keep it, if it was possible at a low cost?

This series of occupations, Portugal as the colonial power, Australia and Japan during the Second World War, and Indonesia from 1975 to 1999, were disastrous from a humanitarian point of view, for East Timor. The loyalty among the Timorese people over time, was generally with Australia. Many Timorese have taken refuge in Australia in various phases of East Timor's modern history.

This loyalty, that many East Timorese felt, was however not reciprocated when Indonesia invaded the East Timor in 1975. How could it be so? Dunn's answer is a combination of Australian lack of independent foreign policy profile at the time—it was seen as more secure to follow its interests in the region and of the United States in particular—and an overwhelming respect for Indonesia's possibility to pose a security threat to Australia.

---

6. Ibid., 44.

Therefore, good relations with Indonesia was for Australia at critical times in the history of East Timor, a priority strong enough for Australia to overshadow its commitment to other principles.

Australia—the richest and economically most influential neighbor of East Timor—was therefore put in a dilemma when the Portuguese government asked for its support in the decolonization of East Timor in 1975. Australia was interested in the petroleum resources available in an unregulated Timor Sea area, and was therefore instead prepared to accept Indonesia's *de facto* (1978) presence—based on occupation—and later a *de jure* (1979) incorporation of East Timor into Indonesia.

As a consequence, Australia and Indonesia later on agreed on a division of the waters between between Indonesia, East Timor, and Australia. The exploration of petroleum resources, which still continues, could then start. The Australian line of policy was fundamentally changed after the Indonesian dictator Suharto was ousted from office in 1998, handing over the presidency to Bacharuddin Jusuf Habibie. When he had expressed the idea that the East Timorese should be given the possibility to choose between a wide autonomy within Indonesia or separation from the country, something we shall look further into below, Australia, as well as the United States and Japan, came to look favorably to the self-determination for East Timor.

For Indonesia the global post-Cold War change of the 1990s did not bode well, it was likely to increase pressure on transparency in Indonesian political life. Many of Indonesia's military actions in East Timor in the 1980s were maybe possible to hide from an international audience, but East Timor was nevertheless an issue that never came to rest—it was the pebble in Indonesia's shoe, as Ali Alatas phrased it once.[7] Also in the 1980s, information came out about Indonesia's terrifying actions in East Timor, even if a comprehensive picture of the period is difficult to get.[8] The 1990s, however, meant a change to this limited exposure and Indonesia had to face the world in a new and different way. During the period of occupation, there was a parallel political development inside and outside of East Timor, not the least in the form of political parties.

---

7. Ali Alatas was foreign minister in Indonesia 1988–1999.

8. During 1975–1976 some 100,000 were killed according to an Indonesian Human Rights organization (Dunn, *East Timor*, ix). A common figure fore the whole 27 years period of Indonesian occupation is 200,000–250,000 killed. This figure amounts to about 1/4 of the total population.

RECONCILIATION AS POLITICS

Party Politics in a Mosaic

The Revolution in Portugal took place in April 1974, ending the regime of Marcelo Caetano, who succeeded Antonio Salazar in 1968, meant also the ending of a several-decades-long military rule of Portugal. East Timor was far away from these events, and they did not imply any immediate change in the Portuguese administration in Dili. For instance, the governor appointed by the military government of Portugal, Colonel Aldeia, stayed in office for yet a few months, in spite of the revolution at home.

For the East Timor elite, the *liruais*[9] as well as the Chinese and Portuguese businessmen, the change was not totally positive, rather the opposite. The relative stability in East Timor was in the end dependent on stability in Portugal, something which so far had been provided by the military regime. Now it was no longer there, however.

We have already noted that East Timor was at the time ill equipped for its prospective independence. Three parties[10] were formed in East Timor in order to deal with this new situation. Their experience of political work was limited and basically relying on the experiences of former members in Portuguese, or later, Indonesian local assemblies in East Timor. What happened was, that during a few weeks in May 1974 three parties were formed in East Timor. The Timorese Democratic Union (UDT), the Timorese Association of Social Democrats (ASDT), and Timorese Popular Democratic Association (Apodeti), all three were established almost at the same time and they came to be the three major political forces for a long time. Later ASDT was succeeded by Fretilin, formed on September 11, 1974. It then became the largest political movements in East Timor, followed by the UDT. The followers of Apodeti never had more then a few hundred as members.[11]

UDT represented land owning, officials, and business groups and became gradually more and more sympathetic to independence the first months of its existence, but argued strongly for a gradual process towards

---

9. A *liurai* is a local, traditional "ruler of the land," in Timor, inheriting the role from earlier kingdoms.

10. The parties were UDT (The Timorese Democratic Union), APODETI (Timorese Popular Democratic Association), and ASDT (Timorese Social Democratic Association).

11. Two other parties were established in this period as well: Kota (Association of East Timorese Heroes) which in that time was in favor of integration with Indonesia, but today is an independence party, emphasizing local traditions, and Trabalhista (labor party), which also had links to Indonesia in the 1970s but is now favoring independence.

a change in any direction. An autonomy arrangement as one step in this process was an early goal for UDT. A major problem for the party was however to distance itself from the colonial regime, which many in the party had served as local officials. In addition, three of the leaders of UDT at the time had served as representatives in the Provincial legislative assembly, in the only legal party in that assembly during the Salazar period (the Acção Nacional Popular).

Fretilin had different roots, it was an independence movement from its first day, and as such had recruited members from many layers of the East Timor society. Its policy had both nationalist and internationalist components, and compared to its main rival, the UDT, it was "more aggressive, disciplined and purposeful" according to Dunn. It went from being a political party to a revolutionary front, but Dunn holds that its leader's attitudes "were attuned more to the socialist aims and aspirations of similar movements in developing countries . . . than those of any communist state."[12]

Apodeti, finally, was clearly in support of integration with Indonesia from the very beginning of its existence. The party program wanted an autonomous integration of East Timor, a construction that was unknown to the Indonesian constitution at the time. The party was to become a link for Indonesian interests into East Timor political life over the years, however the size of the party was always very limited.

The relations between the UDT and Fretilin went in different directions during 1974 and 1975. First, after coming to a point in March 1975 when the two parties in a joint communiqué declared their "intransigent defense of the right of the people to national independence"[13] a change took place. Two months later this cooperation broke down and following another two months, a short civil war broke out in East Timor, in August 1975, between Fretilin and the UDT.

Tension rose to a level in this month, August, to the extent that the UDT launched a coup which according to Walsh[14] was described by Joao Carrascalão, a UDT founder, as an act of "civil disobedience." One explanation to this action on part of UDT has been, that in order to pre-empt an Indonesian invasion, a coup-like take-over in Dili where radical groups within Fretilin should be deported from the island, would calm Indonesia.

12. Dunn, *East Timor*, 57.
13. Walsh, *East Timor Political Parties*.
14. Ibid.

RECONCILIATION AS POLITICS

UDT and (the rest of) Fretilin should then be able to control an ordered transition into independence. Obviously, this was not at all what came to happen.

A few days later and as a response to the UDT coup, Fretilin created Falintil (National Liberation Forces of East Timor) and when they took effective military counter-measures, a small scale civil war broke out. It ended in early September, and had then caused some estimated 1,500 deaths plus refugee flows to West Timor and to Australia.[15]

Falintil and Fretilin gained the upper hand in the political life of East Timor in this way, and on November 28, 1975, Fretilin declared independence for East Timor. This declaration was lasting till December 7, 1975, when Indonesia launched its attack on Dili and made East Timor its 27th province. This was the formal situation until October 1999.

Fretilin was throughout the period, the major movement against the Indonesian occupation. The organization National Council of Maubere Resistance (CNRM) was created in 1979 and it was a way of broadening the resistance against the occupation, inside East Timor. 1981 Xanana Gusmão was elected leader of CNRM. He was later captured and jailed in 1992 by Indonesian forces. CNRM was changed into National Council of Timorese Resistance (CNRT) in 1998, in an attempt to broaden its support even more. The idea was to gather anyone who was opposing Indonesia's military presence in of East Timor. CNRT, as an umbrella organization, was, in connection to the independence process, dissolved in June 2001, in order to open for regular party formations for the new Parliament to come.

The party structure today represents both the old and the new East Timor. The conflict over East Timor's future status, which was the critical issue when the old parties were formed in 1974, was in a way brought into the political agenda and visions of the independent Timor Leste.

THE CRITICAL YEARS OF THE OCCUPATION

The 1990s started with a feeling that, after the fall of the Berlin Wall, continued change was possible, also among the seemingly most locked and rigid situations—such as the occupation of East Timor by Indonesia at the time. Many who were concerned with the East Timor question—academics, politicians, and journalists, mostly in Australia and South East Asia—tended increasingly at this time to hold the view, that the Indonesian occupation

15. Ibid.

of East Timor "could not just continue" as it had done since it started, in December 1975.

There was in the 1990s an awakening internationally of the situation in East Timor. Its long-time struggle was recognized through the Nobel Peace Prize to two of East Timor's leaders—Bishop Carlos Ximenes Belo, Catholic bishop in East Timor, and José Ramos-Horta, international spokesperson for the Fretilin resistance movement and later president.

The single most important move in these critical years of the occupation was of course President Habibie's readiness for a "popular consultation" explained in January 1999, in a surprising, and later on by many in Indonesia highly criticised way. His statement about this possibiility opened for the tripartite talks to come to a conclusion. These talks resulted then in a negotiated agreement on May 5, 1999, which gave the UN responsibility to arrange a referendum. The referendum took place in August 1999 and resulted in 78.5 percent in favor of independence, and 21.5 percent in favor of autonomy within Indonesia.

This outcome of the referendum resulted in widespread looting, killing, and destruction by militia groups in East Timor, who all had Indonesian support. During a few weeks in September 1999 cities and villages all over the country were burnt down, something that lead to quick international reaction and the deployment of 11,000 troops in the International Force East Timor (Interfet)[16] with a mandate to restore security, and from that on prepare ground for the coming of UNTAET. This Mission succeeded Interfet and functioned from fall 1999 to spring 2002 as the governing body of East Timor, up to the country's independence on May 20, 2002.

The conflict was over the occupation by Indonesia and its consequences. It has never been about the Oecussi exclave or over borders, even if typical border problems also have appeared. Neither has the conflict been about religion, although Indonesia has the world's largest Muslim population and East Timor is Catholic. Portuguese missionaries, of course, made East Timor a Catholic territory, something that was made even stronger during the period of Indonesian occupation 1975 to 1999. In essence, however, the religious dimension has not been part of the conflict in any real sense, illustrated by the fact that the first Timor Leste Prime Minister was a Muslim.

---

16. Interfet was composed by troops/personnel from Australia, New Zeeland, Malaysia, the Philippines, and another 14 countries totally.

RECONCILIATION AS POLITICS

The disastrous weeks of violence, looting, and killing in East Timor in September 1999, become for many a symbol of East Timor's history and the nature of its struggle for independence. East Timor was one of many cases in a row of international interventions at the time, through the active involvement of the United Nations in finalizing its state formation process in the period 1999 to 2002 and after that, during a number of years of state-building.

The 1990s proved to be a decisive decade for Indonesia in East Timor. Its annexation was not accepted world-wide, except for Australia which did so in connection to its agreements on oil exploitation with Indonesia. The invasion 1975 had been criticized by the UN Security Council and by subsequent General Assembly resolutions up to 1982, and now and then after that, diplomatically irritating events, such as a letter to the Vatican from the Bishop in Dili, Carlos Belo, strongly criticizing Indonesia's human rights violations, added to the feeling in Jakarta that East Timor was a trouble-making area. Instead, many thought, East Timor should be grateful for the many investments made by Indonesia in East Timor, not the least in its infra-structure. East Timor was at this time Indonesia's poorest part and its investments in the region stood in great contrast to the absent interest for development in East Timor from the Portuguese side.

However, many East Timorese, both with a relatively positive view of a future East Timor integration with Indonesia and those in favor of independence, realized that the methods and behavior of the Indonesian Armed Forces (TNI)[17] was only increasing the general hostility to anything that refers to Indonesia. TNI in practice became a good argument for independence, the challenge for the pro-independence side, was to create a situation where a legitimate expression of the will of the people could take place. In the early 1990s, it was by no means clear how this should take place, given the long period of Indonesian occupation and integration of East Timor into Indonesia, in all respects, and the strong grip held by General Suharto and the Indonesian military had on politics and economics in the country.

Although far away from Lisbon, the fate of a colony is nevertheless shaped from its distant capital. East Timor was not a critical area for Portugal, by no means comparable to Mozambique, Angola, Guinea-Bissau, or Cap Verde. Not even to Goa or Macao. Not to speak about Brazil. From a

---

17. In Bahasa Indonesia language: Tentara Nasional Indonesia.

development point of view, modern services remained an unknown part of East Timor's daily life.

When the Portuguese Carnation Revolution ended the almost fifty-year-long military dictatorship under Salazar, in 1974, the new government set out to leave their overseas possessions. For East Timor this resulted in an unprepared and largely unguided process of internal strife and party formations combined with Indonesian attempts to influence the process. The basic divide came to be between those in favor of integration with Indonesia—often conditioned—and those in favor of self-determination through referendum, which one was sure of should result in independence. Most political parties in East Timor today, in the new parliament of the independent state were formed in this period. There are exceptions, but on the whole, the political divisions in the East Timor society, created in the wake of Portugal's withdrawal, remain to be a living reality in everyday political life. It was this divide that lead to the civil war in 1975.

This leads us to the observation, that this internal division, even if related to the question of East Timor's international status, has had its own dynamic internally in East Timor. This dynamic, the conflicts and the mistrust created by this process, was not part of the issues resolved by the UN referendum in August 1999. In the referendum, East Timor's international status was once and for all decided, and the United Nations, through UNTAET, made this new status a reality. Under the surface, though, was and is a society that lives with its internal problems, many of which are coined in terms set by the 1975 civil war. As we shall see, the referendum made this division even deeper. Under conditions such as those in East Timor 1999, a referendum is the worst possible mechanism from a national unity perspective. This deficiency of the referendum as a conflict resolution mechanism is something that was addressed in many meetings and seminars, before as well as after the referendum had taken place, that are described in this text.

Four Phases in East Timor's State Formation Process

The developments with respect to East Timor took distinct routes from time to time in the critical periods presented here. The years from late 1990s up to independence 2002 can be described in the following way. In brief there were four critical questions that dominated the content of the discussions during each phase. They were:

- 1998 to early 1999: Which options in terms of sovereignty and local rule are there, for small territories, like East Timor? What could a consensus-based transitional process look like?
- Mid-1999: How can divisions about the future on a national level be overcome?
- Late-1999: How can an inclusive political platform for East Timor be constructed given the outcome of the UN referendum/popular consultation?
- 2000: Is there a way of reconciliation in East Timor? And under what conditions can refugees return to East Timor?

THE UNITED NATIONS AND EAST TIMOR

The decolonization and the granting of independence to colonial countries and peoples is a process entrusted with the United Nations. Portugal became a member of the United Nations in 1955 and had already by then experienced almost 30 years of military rule, and almost another 20 more were to come.[18]

In the period of UN membership from 1955 to 1974, Portugal claimed that its overseas territories were an organic part of the country. East Timor, for instance, could therefore not be regarded as a non-self-governing territory in the sense indicated in the UN Charter, article 73. The article states that any government administering such a territory is obliged to give the Secretary-General of the United Nations statistical and other technical information about the situation in the territory.

The purpose of this responsibility is to provide the UN with information with the ultimate objective to be used as a basis for deciding when a given territory is mature enough to exercise its right to self-determination. Portugal's view on this matter changed totally with the new and democratic government in 1974, which accepted the principles of the UN Charter with respect to Article 73, and made subsequent constitutional changes to allow for a process of self-determination in the non-self-governing territories of Portugal. In 1974 and 1975, then, Portugal came to leave all its overseas

---

18. A military coup already in 1926 brought Antonio Salazar into the Portuguese government. He stayed as prime minister until 1968, when he had to hand over the rule of the country to Marcelo Caetano who, in his turn, was overthrown in a leftist, military coup in April 1974.

territories, for instance Guinea-Bissau, Angola, Mozambique, São Tomé and Principe, and East Timor.

East Timor was far away from Portugal, and the country had not resources enough to control and guide developments in East Timor in the months following the 1974 coup. It was not until June 1975 that the UN Special Committee on Decolonization met in Portugal and expressed its view that Portugal had a responsibility to live up to the goals in the Charter of the United Nations where it refers to granting independence to colonial countries and peoples.

This was a late initiative in relation to developments in East Timor, where new parties were formed already in 1974, to which Indonesia had established a clear role and interest. The civil war in East Timor, beginning in August 1975 became soon the best argument for Indonesia to occupy the territory.

The United Nations never accepted, neither in its Security Council resolutions nor in General Assembly resolutions, the acquisition of territory by Indonesia of East Timor. This acquisition was regarded as illegal. The General Assembly took yearly resolutions on the matter up to 1982, always with a critical language of Indonesia's occupation. In the Security Council, however, the United States, Australia, and Japan often voted against resolutions that condemned Indonesia or asked the Secretary-General to investigate the matter. According to the UN decolonization system, however, East Timor was during the Indonesian occupation still a non-self-governing territory, waiting to execute its right self-determination.

As a consequence of the 1982 General Assembly resolution, the then newly elected Secretary-General of the UN, Javier Perez de Cuellar, created a mechanism for consultations between Portugal and Indonesia, under UN auspices.[19] These tripartite talks, as they came to be called, came periodically in the 1980s and 1990s to play an important role, not the least in the final part of the whole process. The talks ended effectively on May 5 1999, with an agreement in New York between Indonesia and Portugal, and with the United Nations as a witness. This was an agreement which set up the terms for a referendum—a "popular consultation"—to be held in East Timor on its future status. The agreement brought an end to 500 years of colonial rule and occupation in East Timor.

The tripartite dialogue was a high-level inter-governmental mechanism. It had no direct representation of persons which lived in the territory

---

19. The resolution calls for the involvement of "all parties directly concerned."

concerned, East Timor. In addition, the dialogue did in the first years only consider humanitarian issues due to Indonesia's refusal to discuss other and more fundamental matters. This was frustrating for East Timor's community leaders in general, both the UDT and Fretilin were critical, and for Fretilin, which claimed political leadership internationally, this was particularly frustrating.

As a way of alleviating this asymmetry, a series of meetings were held in Austria, hosted by the Austrian government and located in Burg Schlaining (1995, 1996) and in Krumbach Castle (1997). The meetings were intended to have an as wide as possible representation of the East Timor society, and could deal with practically any other issue than the ones dealt with within the UN tripartite dialogue. These talks, called the All Inclusive Intra-East Timorese Dialogue (AIETD), were held on the initiative of the UN Secretary-General, with support from Portugal and Indonesia, and with Austria as the host and main sponsor.

Although the meetings in Austria served a purpose by bringing the East Timor civil society, the Church, and many political leaders together—however not Xanana Gusmão who was jailed in Jakarta since 1992—many felt that the most burning issue regarding the future status of East Timor, could not be brought to the table, something an active corridor of conversations could not compensate for. It was however politically impossible to raise such a demand.

A TURNING POINT

A breaking with the relative international silence of the 1970s and 1980s were two actions by the Catholic Church in 1989. First, in a letter from February 6, 1989, Bishop Carlos Ximenes Belo in Dili, describes the suffering of the East Timor people, and requests the United Nations, through its Secretary-General, to "initiate a democratic process of decolonization in East Timor to be realized through a referendum."[20] Second, Pope John Paul II visited Dili in October 1989, something, which brought publicity not only around his visit but also around the demonstrations that took place. Suddenly, during one year, the profile of the East Timor question was raised internationally. This activated the slowly developing tripartite talks.

As a result, it was agreed that an official Portuguese delegation should be given the possibility to visit East Timor, in order to study the situation.

20. Nevins, *A Not-So-Distant Horror*, 73.

The visit was planned to November 1991, and a turning point was about to come.

The Santa Cruz massacre in 1991 was an event that displayed an important side of the nature of the Indonesian occupation during the whole of the 1980s: it was a period during which information from the Catholic Church and from clandestine, individual journalists were the only reliable sources for information about the human rights violations that took place during the time in East Timor. As a result of talks under UN auspices between the governments of Indonesia and Portugal, a parliamentary delegation had been invited to study the situation in East Timor. Just a few days before its arrival, the Indonesian authorities cancelled the visit due to the security situation in Dili.

Following a Sunday morning mass in the Motael Church, Dili, demonstrations took place on the streets between the church and the Santa Cruz cemetery, basically in spontaneous frustration over the cancelled international visit. There were however present some international journalists, flown in for covering the visit, that nevertheless could cover in picture the events, and give accounts of the upfront killing of unarmed Timorese. The number of killed has never been independently secured, official Indonesian figure is 53, different sources in East Timor quote figures more than 250, one source saying 273.[21]

It was—in this, as in other situations as well in East Timor—not the high figures, the death tolls or monstrous sceneries of destruction that caused harm and sympathy in the international opinion, but it was rather the naked violence, inflicted by the strong upon the weak, in a context without any legitimacy neither internationally nor nationally. For the Indonesian government, the Pope's visit and the St. Cruz massacre made the pebble grow into a stone.

These events were coming out of efforts from within East Timor to raise its profile internationally. They described a reality that the East Timorese diaspora, and its prime representative José Ramos-Horta, had expressed in numerous meetings with national leaders, in the UN, and in meetings with grass-roots organizations all over the world, ever since 1975. There was a certain degree—although difficult to uphold—of coordination between the two levels, the internal and external.

Enough time before the difficult years of occupation, a political network had been created, strong enough to formulate itself inside and

---

21. Ibid, 33.

RECONCILIATION AS POLITICS

outside East Timor, and consisting of individuals critical to the occupation by Indonesia. This network could bring events in East Timor and the struggle inside and outside the country to the attention of the 1996 Nobel Peace Prize Committee which the same year awarded Carlos Ximenes Belo, bishop in Dili, and José Ramos-Horta, foreign relations spokesperson for Fretilin, the Peace Prize for their struggle for human rights and the right to self-determination of East Timor.

BREAKING THE MONOPOLY

As we have seen, the AIETD format was not sufficient enough for meeting the needs for an intra-Timorese dialogue on the most pressing questions for the future. At this time, in 1996, the Nobel Prize had not been awarded to two Timorese, the Indonesian President Suharto was still a strong man, and an economic crisis had yet not stricken the Asian countries. Not much seemed possible to change as long as the major regional powers in South East Asia were the same.

There was a growing insight in East Timor, and elsewhere, that there has to come a change—in one way or another. The world was democratizing, military dictatorships had been turned over and civil wars had recently come to an end in both Latin America and Africa, and South Africa had turned away from its apartheid system. Change was possible and East Timor needed to be part of this global wave, although, again, the regional situation was somewhat locked. Would this need for a change mean another war in East Timor, against the occupying power Indonesia? Could it be avoided? Some East Timorese were actively looking for different fora where their reflections and questions could be discussed.

A major achievement in these efforts was the formation of the East Timor Study Group (ETSG), a bi–partisan group for study and policy reflection with the purpose of finding common ground between the different political groupings in East Timor on the question of East Timor's future status, as well as issues related to this. The whole point with the ETSG was its bi–partisan composition. Without this characteristic it had just became yet another political group, but by including a wide scope of opinions it could create a space for dialogue that was not otherwise at hand among East Timorese leaders.

This group of East Timor intellectuals, which represented both sides of the divide—self-determination and pro-integration views, respectively—came gradually together and started actively to search for contacts, knowledge and resources in academic milieus around the world, milieus who could enrich them on the possibilities and alternatives that exist for small territory that is about to develop a new international status. The options were many for the group to consider. Even "independence"—which sounds definitive and well defined—can be designed in very different ways under different conditions. (For instance, some island states in the Pacific are "associated states," due to their limited size,[22] but they are still independent in principle. Also, some autonomies have state-like capacities[23] and in some cases "autonomy" is a transitional status—as in the Oslo Agreement over Palestine.[24] Given this myriad of potential forms for transition of East Timor—into one final status or another—this East Timorese group wanted to develop their understanding of these potential options, besides independence.

TWO DIFFERENT BUT RELATED ISSUES

At this point we can also make an observation of the structure of the conflict in East Timor in this period up to its independence. The United Nations managed the conflict in East Timor from a de-colonization perspective. The issue for the world organization was to safeguard East Timor's right to execute an act of self-determination about its future, and, as it turned out, the UN also became involved in assisting East Timor in doing this. East Timor was one of the last territories to be de-colonized, Western Sahara is at the time of writing a parallel issue. It was East Timor's future international status that was to be determined, in this case through a process of referendum. This type of decisions, obviously, are taken once—as long as it is made within the UN decolonization process.

Besides this historical neccessity, which the referendum can be called, the situation inside East Timor, at the time, was however not conducive for a free and fair political campaign before a referendum. With a history close in time of a short civil war and a subsequent occupation that suppressed all forms of political ativity, there was not a fertile ground the emergence of political awareness and public opinion-making. This is so, because when

22. Examples are Niue and Cook Islands, respectively.
23. An example is Hong Kong.
24. Adding to the list of concepts is "conditional independence," used by the Independent Commission on Kosovo.

RECONCILIATION AS POLITICS

Portugal gave up *de facto* control of East Timor in 1974, the territory was ill-prepared to take its historic destiny into its own hands. Instead a development took place that eventually lead to both a short civil war and a declaration of independence by National Liberation Forces of East Timor (Fretilin), in November 1975. This internal conflict between groups with different approaches to the process of self-determination itself, lead to a conflict pattern originating within East Timor. It is anchored in social, economic, and traditional patterns of values and control, and relates to other dimensions than those that relate directly to the international status issue dealt with by the United Nations.

The UN management of the international status issue did not reduce the internal conflict between groups, parties, and local power holders. As we shall see, it rather had the opposite effect, and it is fair to say that it had to have that effect, due to the very nature of the issue. As noted above, it was an act of self-determination, and that is something which is made "now or never" and which is over "all or nothing." What East Timor experienced, then, was that the overarching issue of the future status of the country materialized during the same years into two types of conflicts, each one on its own level. One of them was the civil war and the killings and scars in the local community from the internal political conflict, emerging right after Portugal's departure, and the other was the campaigning before the referendum over the future status of East Timor. The two levels were dependent on each other, but managed in different ways.

AN EFFECT OF OCCUPATION

The Indonesian occupation has been a deeply formative period for East Timor's society—its way of functioning and identifying itself. Generally, through its resistance against both Portuguese colonialism and in particular the Indonesian military occupation, East Timor became much better organized at the village/regional level than at the national/capital level.

Dealing with problems of food, local security, and—during the armed resistance period—the support of the resistance army in the mountains (Falantil and its predecessors) were activities organized on the basis of local resources, not central. This long period of occupation and resistance made the local community in East Timor a natural basis for social struggle, for the identity and security of the Timorese people. The capital Dili, and the national level in general, represented resources but was also a political/

ideological as well as moral compromise vis-à-vis the occupier. From this perspective it is possible to say, with some support at least, that East Timor has "always" been better organized locally than nationally, throughout decades. This feature of the Timorese society was very helpful also for the reconciliation process that took place after violence had ended and the UN had started preparing for independence. The local mechanisms for reconciliation existed, throughout East Timor's modern history and could therefore, as we will see, be part of the processes towards political reconciliation that East Timor did embark on.

REFERENDUM

The 1999 referendum in East Timor was a way to decide the future status of East Timor. As a method of conflict resolution a referendum is very definitive: it is a "the winner-takes-all" method and it is, in addition to this, intended to provide an outcome "once-and-for-all." Of course, this has its reasons and should not be discussed here. That is history now and the matter for referendum is settled. Even if not everyone—who was involved in the battle in 1999—accepts the outcome, a new reality is created. At the same time, a political culture which reflects the concept of political reconciliation had to be created. The time for practicing reconciliation came with the outcome of the referendum—or "popular consultation" as it was also called.

What role does a democratic system play in this? East Timor began after independence a process towards multi–party democracy. It is easy to link democracy to reconciliation, and to think that democracy in itself is a reconciliatory measure. However, this is not necessarily so. From a conflict resolution point of view, democracy is also a system very different from the referendum's winner-takes-it-all approach. To "win" or to "lose" in a democracy is a relative thing, not an absolute. A victory in a democracy is always temporary, and a loss is therefore also always temporary. There is a new election coming up, with new possibilities and challenges, both to the government and to the opposition. In this way, a democracy is a constant management of, and no final resolution of, the different political aspirations of the people.

This nature of the democratic system makes the role of the political opposition extremely important. Without an active opposition, no living democracy. If a government is based on a solid majority in parliament, the opposition may feel it has no influence. But a passive opposition will in

RECONCILIATION AS POLITICS

practice create a situation which makes the election into a "winner-takes-it-all"-outcome, if it lets the government rule without being challenged on substantial issues. Parliaments have different ways of dealing with this, for instance by having non-government parliament members as chairpersons in the parliament.

If a government has a minority situation, on the other hand, the opposition has one important additional responsibility, besides to be a constructive opposition, that is to be opposition without making the country ungovernable, through constant blocking government proposals, rather than seeking compromise. Of course, also the government then needs to seek compromise—that is natural for any government in a minority situation. All the possible views on this cannot be discussed here. The point here is, that there is a much more important role for the opposition to play than is normally recognized also by many opposition politicians, since all the interest in media and elsewhere is directed towards the government and its actions.

One can say, that in some way it is the opposition rather than the government, that creates the essential qualities of a democracy, in the sense that it creates the debate, the challenging proposals, and the need for accountability of government. Principally speaking, it has a responsibility as great as the government for maintaining the democratic system in good shape, and if the opposition forms coalitions on critical issues, it can be rather influential and decision-making in the parliament can be effective.

When East Timor voted for independence in August 1999, through a majority of 78,5 percent, it entered a process where all the historic legacies described above somehow should be taken care of: the short civil war between the two parties in the wake of Portugal's "disappearance" from East Timor (with all the antagonisms that this brought into the civil society), the long period of clandestine work and secret resistance activities inside East Timor, the need to find a way to survive on a daily basis with a strong Indonesian presence in East Timor, strong enough to make a cease-fire not only militarily understandable but politically useful for creating a basis for a peaceful change in the long-term. This meant, that if political reconciliation was to come in East Timor, it needed to deal with both the *internal* conflict and its tension, and the *international* question—administrated by the United Nations—over what shall be the future status of East Timor—autonomy within Indonesia or independence? And finally, whatever outcome of these two levels and processes, the neighbor in the north of Timor Leste would always be Indonesia—a regional superpower.

9

A Reflection on Timor Leste

Lewis Coser makes an important observation in his classical book *The Functions of Social Conflict* about the effect of overlapping interests between members of major social groups—the crisscross effect. Societies with many groups with different views, organized in political parties or in other ways, can be very stable. A community may very well stay together as a unit, according to Coser, as long as there are at least some overlapping interests on at least some issues. These issues are then crisscrossing over different social boundaries.

The "trick" is that even if there are many divisions, there is also at least somebody that shares you opinion, whatever it is about, and even if you disagree on all other things in life. This means de facto a reduction of tension in a society. For instance, it is often said that the peaceful relations between the cantons in Switzerland is due to the fact that among Catholics there are both French and German speaking (and also Italian speaking persons), and among Protestants there are as well Frenchmen and Germans. So, neither religion nor language can bring all cantons together into two groups pitted against each other. In the same way, many parties in East Timor do not necessarily lead to divisions in the society, even if it looks as if there were many groups divided between each other. There is—as far as is possible to see—no fundamental rift in the East Timor society, that can divide the society totally. Instead, in different regions in East Timor, there are persons with different views, whether about the 1999 referendum, about language, religion, economy or class issues. This points to a diversity of rather serious and anchored opinions, which means that no fundamental division is likely to develop.

RECONCILIATION AS POLITICS

A case in point where this overlapping was largely missing for long periods is Northern Ireland. A large number of very important dimensions of life—economy, schooling, access to services, and political influence, just to mention a few that were all defined by one single line of division—that between Catholics and Protestants. The two sides were divided on all for them important dimensions: religion, social and economic situation, political opportunities, and historic connection to Dublin and London, respectively. The overlapping issues were very few, probably the most important overlapping aspect was, and is, the economy where the EU, plus Great Britain and the Republic of Ireland, have made enormous efforts to keep unemployment low, investment high and create an environment that makes people survive economically and see a future also in Northern Ireland. This was a basis for the peace agreement in 1998, often called the Good Friday Agreement.

What political reconciliation can do, is to have an impact on such divisive community group relationships. Political reconciliation can contribute to the crisscrossing of relationships over former, or traditionally well established, fault lines in a community.

Therefore, it is not necessarily a problem for a community if it consists of many different groups, with different priorities and goals, as long as they relate to other groups on at least a few dimensions. It is easy to talk about countries with many different languages, cultures, or socially different groups as problematic areas. In a study of Timor Leste, this author made the following tentative illustration of some social structures in the country. The purpose is not to go into details in this here, it is presented as an illustration to how the crisscross effect can work, since the fault lines indicated in the figure do not create one or two major divisions crossing through the whole country. Instead they stretch over horizontal as well as vertical lines of division. In addition, an individual person can belong to several groups, with different levels of attachment to each group. As a totality this creates bonds between many different groups and local identities, which creates stability as long as there are at least one or a few overarching identities where everyone can join.

A Reflection on Timor Leste

Figure 7. Structural dividing lines in Timor Leste

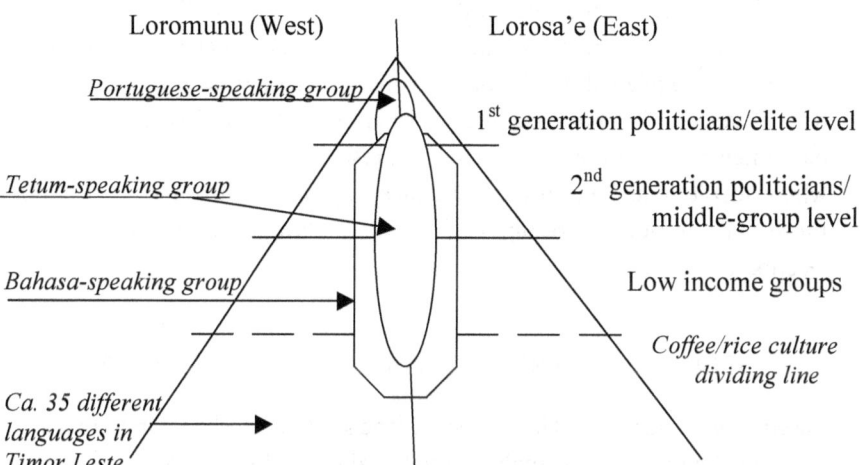

From Figure 7, which is indicating structural dividing lines in Timor Leste, it is possible to understand how no group is big enough for dividing the country. It is natural for any state-building project to keep divisions low, to stress national unity and to reduce the possible impact of divisions. This discussion is not an argument against such a policy, but the point is, that there is a level when interests that are overlapping each other into a pattern of seemingly very difficult dividing lines, it could actually serve stability. If such differences are displayed in a peaceful and enriching way, they could actually contribute to the diversity and richness of a country in a very positive way.

A somewhat similar argument can be made with respect to political parties. An advantage with many small parties, in the outset of a democratization process of a country, is that they can mobilize individuals and create an interest in political activity to a higher degree than a few national parties can. Many small parties may not have a nation-wide organization, and have only regional or local ambitions. If they try to gradually establish themselves on a larger scale, it is basically a good thing for the spread of knowledge, awareness and interest in the political system. On the other hand, there is a risk that the parties remain geographically and socially limited. Their "smallness" is then a problem since they consist of so small

RECONCILIATION AS POLITICS

social networks, that persons who are potentially interested to relate to them, feel that they cannot do that, since the party is too "local."

The fundamental aspect of diversity is how it is handled: it can lead to an all-against-all situation. This leads nowhere, any party fighting such a political struggle will fail before its voters. It can also lead to a situation of gradual coalition-building, first on one, then on more issues. For those parliamentarians interested in achieving results, this is a fascinating game, where ideology and interest are balanced against each other. Also here: those that can point to results will have something to say, when the next election comes.

SECURITY AND RECONCILIATION IN TIMOR LESTE

Based on experiences in Timor Leste, Francisco Guterres[1] has since long argued for the relevance of analyzing political reconciliation from a security perspective. The obvious reflection on this, from an instrumental perspective, is to say that if political reconciliaton means a more stable society, that is also a more secure society, than we would be interested in identifying which elements that provide such a linkage.

From the view of a broader security concept, another reflection is important: is there a risk of negative security impact of a political reconciliation if it becomes too overt, revealing and threatening for some groups, and therefore a security threat in itself? How much of new or openly presented information can a society receive at each given point in time, without splitting up and turning violent? That is maybe a rhetoric question more than analytical, but it conveys an issue that needs to be discussed.

The concepts of reconciliation and security, respectively, belong to traditionally separated spheres of society—the individual and the state levels. This separation naturally influences any view on the utility of political reconciliation as a security-related process. Is it meaningful to understand reconciliation among political actors as something more than a nice and harmless activity, which no one can have doubts about, since it has no impact on the realities of a power-oriented society? Or are we dealing with substantial political changes through a new mechanism?

"For East Timor, reconciliation is identical with security," writes Guterres,[2] a year after independence, and during a critical period of the

1. Guterres, *Reconciliation in East Timor*.
2. Ibid.

consolidation of the new Democratic Republic of Timor Leste. In the years leading up to independence, reconciliation was in East Timor a significant political concept developed to deal the different opinions entrenched among groups and parties stemming mainly from the civil war, a war which gave Indonesia a political possibility to intervene in 1975.

The civil war was fought in the wake of Portuguese unilateral withdrawal and which was done without any preparation for a peaceful change of status of the territory of East Timor, which at the time was on the UN list of non self-governing territories.

Guterres writes:

> There were two main streams in East Timor already the first months after the 1999 violence. First, there was the view that reconciliation should be based on the return of refugees as well as on the application of "justice for those to whom justice ought to be done." This means that reconciliation should be carried out in a spirit of forgiveness and temporarily burying the past in order to support a program of repatriation of refugees. By temporarily burying the past, East Timor would encourage the return of refugees, including the real perpetrators. Perpetrators will be welcomed back to East Timor and be given a chance to settle themselves before being brought to the court. Many resistance leaders, including Xanana Gusmão and some victims of the violence as well, advocated such a position. This position was well received by the militias and by other supporters of the pro–autonomy. Secondly, there was the position that justice should come first or together with reconciliation. All perpetrators—regardless of the nature of their involvement in the recent violence—should be brought to court. Reconciliation is only for those who never committed any violence in East Timor. Many victims, some international and local NGO's, and members of the young generation in East Timor advocated this position.

This quotation illustrates the instrumental use of reconciliation in a political context and it cuts straight through some fundamental moral issues—justice first, and then reconciliation, or reconciliation first, and then justice?

The view that all refugees should be allowed to return back, and at a later stage the question of legal responsibility should be brought up, was not only developed as a gesture of embracing all nationals, but also an expression of concern due to the weakness, not to say non-existence, of a nationally based, effective court system at the time. It would have been through international courts that the legal processes would have to pass, had they taken place at all. If the second view was adopted, and at the same time, international courts would not have been able to prosecute all (which is what happened later on) then the refugees would not have had any chance of a legal return back home.

Was it at all necessary to include a reconciliation perspective into a critical political situation? From this author's experience, "reconciliation"—for what it means in the local Timorese culture—was one of the few concepts that was overarching the political sphere and thus could formulate a picture of the society that everyone in principle could understand irrespective of political background. The idea was, that if a new nation should be built, it cannot be done upon shattered or polarized political dreams, but on a common idea—here it became: "if we reconcile, we will find a common future, if not, this small country will be divided and occupied once more."

EAST TIMOR EXAMPLES OF A COMPREHENSIVE PROCESS

This fairly long history and all its events and major structural challenges, are all building up to a moment of conditions for political reconciliation to take place on several levels in the Timorese society and in different ways. Let us return to Table 1 with four aspects of peace processes from chapter 1 and see what examples the East Timor process include, that can fill in each of the four squares.

A basic approach to processes of confidence-building, social reconstruction and reconciliation is the mutually supporting role that the types of acts and processes play illustrated in Figure 8.

Figure 8. Examples from Timor Leste of a comprehensive peace process

	Political level	Individual level
Legal Aspect	1. UN referendum on future status	2. UN Serious Crimes Unit
		↑
		5. Badame Process
		↓
Moral Aspect	3. Leader's apologies	4. Commission for Reception, Truth and Reconciliation (CAVR)

If we begin with the legal level, the UN-arranged referendum (1) in August 1999, over the future status of East Timor, is the historic equivalent to a peace agreement. The conflict in East Timor had to be settled in this way, if the territory's right to self-determination should be respected. The outcome, 78,5 percent in favor of independence and 21,5 percent in favor of an autonomy arrangement within Indonesia, was clear enough to create an unambiguous interpretation of the result. The outcome was binding to Indonesia and Portugal who had signed an agreement on May 5, 1999, over the referendum (called "popular consultation") to be held with the assistance of the United Nations. In line with the outcome, in October 1999 East Timor ceased to be a province of Indonesia.

While this was the international dimension of the East Timor conflict, square two (2) on the legal dimension shows the UN Special Panels/ Serious Crimes Unit as an example of the legal responsibility that individuals globally can no longer be sure of avoiding, in the wake of armed conflict and war—if they have committed serious violations of human rights and comparable acts. The UN Serious Crimes Unit was established after the UNTAET mission took over in 2000 and was working with cases up to 2005.

RECONCILIATION AS POLITICS

The UN Serious Crimes Unit was given the mandate to investigate the most *serious* forms of crimes during the conflict, such as genocide, crimes against humanity, war crimes, torture, murder, and rape/sexual offences. *Less serious* crimes, such as minor assault, theft, arson, and killing of animals (livestock) were channeled through the Commission for Reception, Truth and Reconciliation which could refer the matter to a *community reconciliation process*, as part of the traditional Badame system of settling conflicts. This local process was made a formal part of the UN legislation that gave a legal basis for the whole system, in the first place. A person who had fulfilled the requirements of the community based reconciliation process could obtain a document that declared the legal validity of his/her participation concerning the acts that were part of the process.

If we turn to square number three (3), the role of leaders for expressing national policies and sentiments is critical for the acceptance of reconciliatory gestures and actions. The role of some political leaders for such a policy cannot be underestimated. In the case of South Africa, Nelson Mandela is obviously a given example in South Africa, and for Timor Leste—both in its pre- and post-independence politics—Xanana Gusmão developed a strong view along the same lines, based on East Timor's cultural traditions and security political needs of today.[3]

A critical example if this view is the openness of the CNRT leadership, which paved the way for the return of moderate East Timor People's Front (BRTT)[4] and other leaders to political work in East Timor. This took place on the national level and was a result of a series of meetings (for instance in Singapore, Tokyo, Bali) and much communication in between. This restructuration of confidence and mutual trust between former enemies, was crucial for the security and general acceptance of the public of the returning politicians—they were the politicians that had lost the referendum. This group, consisting of East Timorese politicians who had propagated for an autonomy within Indonesia, rather than independence, were Timorese people who simply had lost a democratic and in all respects fair referendum. Their return home, to East Timor, was actually much more dangerous for their personal security than was the home-coming of representatives of the winning side. Therefore, establishing a firm policy towards reception

---

3. Ishizuka, *Impact of UN Peace-Building*.

4. In Bahasa Indonesia: Barisan Rakyat Timor Timur, a moderate pro-autonomy group.

and welcoming of the losers was an important security issue for the winning side, as well as it had a humanitarian dimension.

The fourth square, (4), with its example of the CAVR is the obvious example. It was set up in 2001, and started working in 2002. Formally it was an independent statutory body mandate, established by UNTAET in July 2001. Its work was to cover the period from 1974 to 1999 and contained a number of activities, where the most important one was truth seeking and facilitating a community reconciliation process (already existing in East Timor) within the CAVR reconciliation process. The CAVR was dissolved in 2005 and produced a 2,800 page report, Chega!, based on over 8,000 individual statements from all over the country. Statement-taking and verification of events was a key task for the CAVR besides the arrangement of public hearings.

The acceptance of the validity of the community reconciliation process for the national, formal legal system puts the CAVR in a position somewhat different from many other truth commissions, and this is indicated with the name "Badame" at position five (5) in the table. "Badame" is a name for a traditional, non-formal reconciliation process on community level in East Timor/Timor Leste. This puts CAVR in the same, very unique category of truth commissions with some sort of legal mandate, South Africa is the other example. While the South African commission had a process for granting amnesty, this was not the case in Timor Leste. Amnesty was never an option in the community based processes under the CAVR period. What is worth noting is, that Badame, and the community reconciliation processes were before, during and after the violence in 1999 living and practiced mechanisms for solving community-conflicts. It is not a reconstructed tradition or a conglomerate of different local practices but also today, a visitor to Timor Leste could follow such a process, in a village or even in the capital Dili.

WHAT ROLE FOR THE COMMISSION OF TRUTH AND FRIENDSHIP INDONESIA-TIMOR LESTE?

East Timor became an independent state in 2002, named the Democratic Republic of Timor Leste. This young republic had, and has, a large part of its younger population speaking the language of its former occupant—Bahasa Indonesia. The contacts between the two countries will continue and hopefully increase as time goes by and relations are defined on another basis than a troubled history. It is not difficult to understand if a small country would argue that it is not a viable option to continue on the level of confrontation, political conflict, and strained relations with, in this case, Indonesia under such circumstances. This is so in particular since Timor Leste's neighbor in the south, Australia, is equally interested in improved relations with Indonesia, and has no interest in supporting an intransigent Timor Leste, with a more narrow agenda. But does this imply, that Timor Leste and Indonesia have a common interest in establishing a commission for truth and friendship, just a few years after their violent confrontations?

If not pushing for the extradition to Timor Leste of Indonesian militaries with a dark history in the country, would that necessarily imply a process of truth and friendship with an occupier?

As we have seen, Timor Leste was in its very first years as independent state pursuing a policy in strong support of political reconciliation without pressing for legal justice. Reconciliation is relation-building on a community level much more than exacting legal justice between individuals, and this was more important than anything else. And in addition—if it produces security for the country, why not, the reasoning seem to be?[5]

Given such a point of departure, how can we understand the work of, in this case the Commission of Truth and Friendship Indonesia-Timor Leste (CTF), from a long-term and peace-building perspective? We have noted in previous chapters that democracies don't go to war against each other. There are two competing explanations for this: one is, that decision-making in democracies take too long time, and does therefore not allow for the quick and surprising action that any successful war requires in theory (an instrumental explanation), and the other explanation says that people in democracies simply don't expect a democratic neighbor to go to war, since they both have given up the idea of using arms as a method of conflict resolution (a normative explanation). Neither Indonesia nor Timor Leste have strong democratic traditions, but for different reasons, and the question is to what extent each of the two explanations are applicable—should the countries be able to avoid conflict and develop more friendly relations.

It can be argued that the CTF is in itself a good and interesting example of how governments on the basis of developing and shared norms, deal with a sensitive and potentially problematic dimension of their relations. Instead of trusting existing common norms, the CTF can be seen

---

5. Ishizuka, *Impact of UN Peace-Building*.

as a way of creating shared norms. In an interesting study on the topic of interstate reconciliation after war a comparison is made between the case of China and Japan, on the one hand, and Germany and Poland, on the other.[6] China and Japan has so far failed to establish friendly relations after the Second World War, but Germany and Poland, has been able to do so. The question is then: how could this be explained?

The most important explanation of the difference between the two cases is in this study, that the political leaders in Poland and Germany during many years (i.e., a decade in the Cold War era) after the Second World War—and contrary to their colleagues in China and Japan—did not use history for their *internal political agenda*. They did not develop their own official myths about "the other country" and its responsibility and alleged evil actions in the past. Instead they let historians on both side find out as much as possible of what happened—on both sides.

The author of the study then concludes by saying, that the most effective way to prevent egoist, national myths is for two countries to form a common historical interpretation of their common past.

While the purpose of the CTF may have been to bring into light a large number of serious human rights violations and other serious acts, its normative and long-term effect may very well be on another level. The commission was not able to bring individuals to legal processes, and its mandate was severely criticized by the United Nations and human rights organizations, since it included a possibility of granting amnesty (which it did not use). The report of the commission makes it more different for anyone who wants to use myths and stories about what happened in East Timor, as part of an internal political agenda. This is, in my reading, the most important contribution of the commission.

Governments have relations, as have peoples through their various organizations (NGOs, religious organizations, etc.). The figure stresses that arrows should rather go either *horizontally* or *vertically* than *diagonally*, which could cause confusion—for instance if a government tries to influence another state's people directly, over the shoulder of that country's government. Let's reflect more on this below.

---

6. Yinan, "Overcoming Shadows."

RECONCILIATION AS POLITICS

SOME STRUCTURAL RELATIONS

Can there be political reconciliation between groups/countries who have "un-reconciled" leaders? What type of reconciliation do leaders agree on—if they at all are reconciling?

An answer needs to begin with, that leaders always assess the possibility to "trust," or to "do business" with the other side, when meeting. When the "chemistry" is of bad quality, even the best of agreements may fail to be signed. As in all other roles for leaders, their personal relations cannot, and should not, be decisive for the fate of their respective groups or countries. Good relations helps, and bad can be a disaster. Political reconciliation, however, is most likely something that leaders can pave the way for, but irrespective of their personal relations, they cannot impose it—that would be contrary to the whole idea of reconciliation.

Both vertical and horizontal relations are important for leaders. One may wonder which relations that are most important among the following possibilities, as described in Figure 9.

Figure 9. Vertical and horizontal reconciliation relations

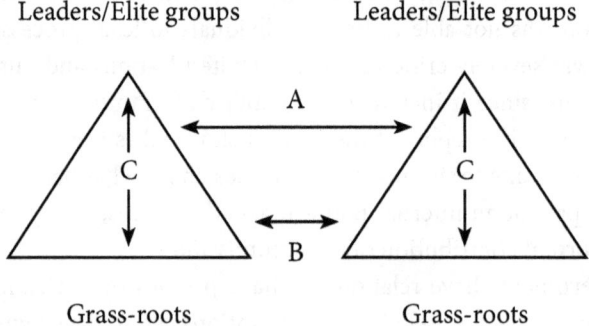

What the figure illustrates on a general level is that reconciliation between two groups, or two individuals, who are in symmetric relations to each other, is fundamentally different from other types of reconciliation. This is important to keep in mind, since relations normally have at least some asymmetry in themselves. The ideal model of a symmetric relationship hardly exists anywhere, neither in personal, nor international relations. It is the letters A and B in Figure 9 that illustrate symmetric relations between two groups (or sides) in conflict, whether on grass-roots level or on elite level.

Letter C indicates a different relation. Here the conflict is *internal*, within a group itself. The issues are then to be dealt with by persons who will continue living with each other. For the most common armed conflict today, the civil war—as mentioned many times previously—this is a real challenge. If an army or a guerilla group commit serious crimes against a population there is, besides the crimes in themselves, also an *asymmetric* confidence problem to be sorted out. The fact that a perpetrator continues to stay in the country is particularly challenging. It may be more easy to deal with an oppressive occupier that leaves the country, than an internal army who has been oppressive but which stays on—with or without a cleaning of the worst cases, "lustration"—in one's own country.

A third type of relation, which is not indicated in Figure 9 is the problem of how a leader or elite group from one side relates to the grass-roots of the other side. For instance, how can a leader of a country relate to the people of another country, in a way of confidence and trust, after violent relations, maybe for years?

It is fairly obvious, and therefore easy to say, that *truth* is a condition for each one of the relations—whether internal or between groups. But truth is a flexible concept both in relation to *what* content should be covered in order for truth to be present, and in relation to *who's perspective* is necessary to include for truth to appear. Nevertheless, an imperfect but seriously made attempt is often respected as a contribution to "truth-building." For responsibility as well as the levels of "compensation" and "meeting" to be realized, all sorts of truth—from factual information of common experiences to personal interpretations of unique phenomena—may therefore be helpful and an improvement of conditions for political reconciliation. For asymmetric relations to be reconciled on a political level, the leaders need to be both factually correct about the past, and as an attitude of trust for the future, also be able to show by deeds that they have fundamentally changed their "mind" or at least their policy.

That means that sometimes we will see a *conditional* relationship between the levels: one level would not care about reconciliation until one or more other levels have done so. "I don't need to take an initiative unless the elite does" could be a typical expression.

It would equally well be interesting to discuss if there is any *causal* link between one type of political reconciliation structure, and another: reconciliation between elites do in fact spark similar initiatives by other categories. If so, it could be explained in many ways—but following the elite is in itself a common behavior in many situations of choice.

RECONCILIATION AS POLITICS

Finally, an *associational* relationship is probably what we mostly will see. Certain patterns of regularity appear between certain structural relations—and maybe also methods—and these regularities need to be explained, normatively and/or instrumentally.

DIFFERENT CONTENT AT DIFFERENT TIMES

Before we conclude this chapter, we will make an observation about intra- and intergenerational political reconciliation. Table 9 illustrates how different parts of a reconciliation process have impact during different periods, if not generations. It all begins with truth-telling, and the truth-telling can continue over generations—new facts can literally be brought into the light long after the event which they tell about (exhumations). The reconciliation aspect is however always present, it is a lived experience among people. If not, it either belongs to history or does not exist. Finally, there is in all political reconciliation processes a moment of orientation towards the future: "non-repetition," "securing human rights and a new order," and similar expressions, expected to guarantee that a grim past will not come back. Planning for that is often materialized in the form of museums, truth commissions, and memorial sites.

Table 9. Reconciliation and trust-building processes over time

	Intra-generational	Inter-generational
Past	Truth-telling	Exhumations (case: Spain)
Present	Truth-telling	Re-interpretation (often culturally expressed)
Future	"Non-repetition"; Shared view of history; Cooperation and friendship based on common interests; Democratic practice improving	Monuments/museums; Cases laid to rest; Individual comfort

10

Political Reconciliation— A Contribution to Politics?

We have up to this point reflected on conceptual and practical dimensions of a relative newcomer in the conceptual toolbox for peacebuilding on the national and international level. In this final chapter we shall bring together some observations and put them before the question if there is a contribution, and therefore some potential utility, in the concept of political reconciliation. Let us begin by reminding ourselves about a few important observations.

The first observation we can make is that a process involving individual experiences requires time and respect for the individual's pace for, in this case dealing with the past. This is particularly important when dealing with a society where many have made existentially significant and often life-changing experiences.

Secondly, we have noted that although a conflict is settled, maybe in an agreement, there are most likely remaining issues which individuals and groups feel more or less concerned about and which will impact on their assessment whether political reconciliation is realistic and desirable at a certain point in time, a point which may not overlap with that of the authorities.

Thirdly, in a brief observation we noted that societies that need political reconciliation the most, are likely to have the least of resources available for managing such a process. This is an irony in one sense, but highly understandable. We have also noted that even if this is the case, and many societies realize that a process of political reconciliation may not be better than any other administrative effort on national level, this has not deterred anyone to refrain.

Fourthly, the idea of reconciliation, as outlined in a peace agreement, can take many shapes. Comprehensive peace agreements, as we have noted in the first chapter, are today regularly including at least some mechanism that is dealing with the past, whether through the concepts of "truth," "historical clarification," or "reception," and "reconciliation." Such mechanisms are important, but as all other political processes—another will take over interest relatively soon. In order to be remembered, some institutional basis for remembering is necessary.

With very few exceptions so called truth and reconciliation commissions have all had only political and moral significance, they have been without legal powers. The most well-known commission, probably, the South African Truth and Reconciliation Commission, was an exception from this rule with its capacity to grant amnesty through a particular procedure. Again, this is not what we find when reading about a very large majority of commissions.

The general problem that is in focus through this development is, we can assume, as old as war itself. Also the morally most justifiable wars result in suffering and death as well as material devastation. Historically, war compensation was only paid by states to states, but the idea that individual persons should be, or have the right to be, compensated after conflict and war is a relatively new one. Basically it is a recognition of the increasingly stronger place of the individual in general in the modern society and in international legal terms, including not the least the development of international human rights and human rights law. It can be seen as a recognition and consequence of a state that is unable to defend human rights, maybe through trespassing itself the moral boundary between the state and the individual, when pursuing conflict.

The contribution to politics is of course dependent on how we define "political reconciliation" and how it is practiced. A main idea in this book has been to focus what is specific for reconciliation, in comparison to, for instance, forgiveness or conflict resolution. The mixture of these concepts, in research and analysis as well as in political practice, is not beneficial for the process, we have argued, and it does not really make it possible to utilize the potential of neither reconciliation nor, for instance, forgiveness.

Our definition of political reconciliation is that it is a social process where harm, resulting from political violence, is repaired in such a way that basic trust is established between victims, perpetrators, and the society at large. This process should then have components which result in a mutual recognition of the two sides, of the other side's experience as important for their own self-understanding. From this follows a self-interest in compensating and interest in the non-repetition of a harmful historic past.

The driving force behind the utility of "reconciliation" is its capacity to reduce polarization and therefore tension, by focusing on the parties' conscious expansion of their horizons. Not that they should fuse horizons, but expand them in order to orientate themselves better in a moral and political landscape. From that new vintage point they will be able to see the importance of the Other for their own life story. Having passed that threshold, the ensuing steps are morally logical and politically already practiced. This is the contribution from "political reconciliation" should it be employed in a conscious way.

RECONCILIATION AS "PRE-POLITICS"

Politics is not "all"—in life or in the world as whole. As an early and general reflection on the relationship between politics and reconciliation, an observation can be that reconciliation is not a "political process" of traditional type (including its 'violent continuation', as Clausewitz would say). It is rather a "pre-political" process in the sense that it is a de facto recognition that "politics" has failed to produce an acceptable social situation, and that in order to avoid (total) social destruction or implosion, and in order to produce conditions for a more acceptable development, one or another form of "reconciliation" is necessary.

Reconciliation, as a political process, gives space and provides incentives for the restoration of individual and group relations broken on the basis of political conflict. It aims at adding a "relational," "informational," and "reflectional" contribution to the political process and the security dimensions of a peace process. By "relational" is meant that relations that have been broken due to a political conflict are restored, by "informational" is meant that as part of reconciliation comes telling one's own truth, recognizing that there is not one single truth or interpretation of an event. This truth telling is the basis for the acknowledgement of injustice, of suffering and of the restoration of human dignity. Finally, by "reflectional" is meant the necessary component of self-reflection and a show of a new and different attitude on part of the perpetrator. This can happen in legally relevant as well as symbolic situations. As we have seen, it is however not always a black-and-white situation when it comes to "who is a perpetrator." Therefore, a moment of self-reflection among all is a very helpful experience in a process called reconciliation.

WHEN IS POLITICAL RECONCILIATION ACHIEVED?

Measures undertaken in a society after armed conflict, based on concepts such as transitional justice, reconciliation, reparation, rebuilding etc., indicate in themselves that there is a limit, an end, to the time when such measures should be necessary. It is important to ask the question: when is political reconciliation achieved? Or, to make the question more precise: when is a society reconciled to the degree that special measures for reconciliation to happen are not necessary for a peaceful future development of that society?

Commissions for truth and reconciliation are short-term projects, often by intent since it has been an idea accompanying such commissions, that they should be intensive, all-encompassing and in-depth—a controlled metamorphosis for the country. This is probably the only politically acceptable approach, a period of moral state of emergency. After that, things should be "normalized," if not normal. Of course, this is an idealistic expectation. It fits the interest among those who have access to power of some sort, but for those without voice, for the victims, and for those accused whose cases are pending in the courts, the reality is quite different.

From this argument we may conclude that neither a truth commission nor other institutional mechanisms are likely to be useful indicators for answering the question for this chapter. Instead, ways and means to identify qualitative aspects of social relations seem necessary.

At this point, we should make the observation that political reconciliation is not a necessary condition for a peaceful development of a society or country after armed conflict—as long as we talk about peace in a negative sense, at least. Many countries still wait for a reconciliation process, even if a particular war or armed conflict has ended: Northern Ireland, Sri Lanka, Lebanon, Mozambique, Nepal—just to mention a few.

Asking the question "when to stop" is an indirect way of asking: "what do you intend to achieve by a political reconciliation process?" Is it avoid violence in the streets, or to create a platform for intergroup relations on community level, or to make people trusting government again—or maybe all three of these?

As we remember from the definition of political reconciliation in previous chapters, one element is about the need for an individual or group to realize that its own picture of truth, or its own view of its place in society, may not be the only relevant one for that individual, or for that group. Instead, to realize the importance of the Other also for me, or for us, who used to be in conflict, that is the first and necessary element of reconciliation, it is claimed in this book. Through this insight, the perspective is shifting, the analysis enriched with new angles, and an *acknowledgement* of the other side is beginning to take place.

From this observation follows, that when individuals and groups who previously were in conflict, can relate to each other in a peaceful way (no violence) and with a certain degree of mutual respect (no hate speech or denigrating comments by default), then we have reached a point when relations have a chance to be improved through established and permanent mechanisms in a society, from schools and cultural institutions to civil society organizations and political parties.

Someone may need to monitor the development of intergroup relations in newly peaceful societies, and eventually introduce specific means to avoid tension or misunderstandings, but this is what may be necessary also in well-established and generally peaceful societies. The conclusion here is then, that when groups accept their mutual importance for each other in their description of their society (which is not to socialize or create bonds that not were there before the conflict), that society has reached a level of reconciliation that has changed the direction of its development.

The second criterion in the definition was about reparation. A society that accepts reparation for some but not for all (because all may not be victims), knows its history and thus realizes why this redistribution of resources takes place. What under different conditions would have been regarded as unjust treatment by broad layers in a society is in a reconciled accepted because it is part of the self-understanding about *what is necessary to do*—not only for the victims but also for the stronger group's self-perception.

A third criterion in the definition was about non-repetition of the past. This leads us towards measuring views and perceptions about the past—maybe not the "good old days," but the "old days"—how are they regarded after a reconciliation process? *Was it better before*? If broad layers in a society believes that "it was better in the past" while at the same time a large part of the country and its population was involved in ongoing, open warfare or fighting, it indicates a serious split, or division within the country, and one may seriously question if that country as a whole has reached a point of political reconciliation.

RECONCILIATION AS A META-STORY

Since reconciliation—also political reconciliation—means that both sides leave the original point of conflict and gradually integrates the perspective of the other side(s), it is a process that in a longer perspective not only leaves the ground of conflict, but also leaves the ground of one's own old views and perspectives. A long-term process of reconciliation creates a meta-story about itself, that is, a new story which is about the old memory and story about what happened in the past. This is basically a process of distancing oneself from the past, not as a form of rejection or repression of memory but as maturing over fate in life through looking at one's own life as from a distance.

In order for such a process to take place, a few things are likely to be helpful. The first is, that a person should try to remember also without activating the emotional energy that may always accompany certain memories. This is such an easy thing to say or write, but those who have gone through long-term processes of reconciliation can maybe give a better hint about what this all means. It is a reason for remembering, and not forgetting, while at the same time be reconciling.

A second help is of course that other parts of life unfold in a way that does not amount to equally or almost equally hard life conditions after a reconciliation process as there were before. If nothing changes, the basis for changing perspective on life is also seriously limited.

A third help is if the original constellations of parties and interests have been changed, and/or dissolved or in other ways act and appear differently as compared to before. Such changes, if only superficial, makes it easier to re-assess and redefine situations and one's own place in the room.

One can say, that as long as a victim or perpetrator, wishing to reconcile, is remaining in the conflict, "on ground" so to speak, that process of reconciliation is a direct one, and it is directly related to the actual conflict. At one point, however, this connection to original conflict is lost— maybe in the sense, that the importance of the original conflict has either disappeared or transformed itself into new priorities or new formations of interests. Thus, the old patterns of thought and action have no place to go. A meta-story about reconciliation and about the old time, can be developed, thus taking forward the dissociation from the past that began with the first steps towards leaving one's own defensive cocoon in the original conflict, to an open and a wider attitude where positions in the old conflict is no longer carrying the sense of safety it once did.

Political reconciliation is the beginning of a process that in the end takes the form of a *meta-story* about events and times in the past. All forms of reconciliation begins in the empirical world. That's why truth is a key. All other activities in a reconciliation process—as has been argued in this study—are dependent on truth, its form and content. The story about what happened, who was involved, and when something took place, is indispensable information for victims as well as for all others who want an understanding of the past.

In this respect, political reconciliation and conflict resolution begin in the same reality, the same issues and events, but the focus of the political conflict can still be upon other aspects than those that need to be treated in a reconciliation process. Therefore, reconciliation can and should not be seen or used as an alternative to conflict resolution, and vice versa: the settlement of a conflict through resolving the core issues may still leave serious and traumatic issues behind. Some of them could very well be strong enough to jeopardize any political agreement, in a short or longer perspective.

Why a meta-story? Through a changing attitude, a wider outlook, and redefined relations to others, a person or a group that is reconciling takes on a world-view which is less polarized, wider in scope and therefore more reflective than previously. This leads to more understanding and a wider perspective, something that requires a certain distance. A new life story is unfolding, a story that brings its owner to a point of reference outside the hurting memories. In the end it becomes a new story about the old one.

Such a process reflects how redefined relations to parties is means redefining the reading of what those parties did in the past. The connection between "truth" and "view of the other" is a critical connection. It is by no means exclusive to political reconciliation processes, it plays an active role in everyday decisions and opinions about other persons, including friends and family members. A reconciliation process addresses this particular aspect of human relations, and invites them to reflect on who the Other is.

Maybe someone else than you believed? To take that step is decisive and the story about the walk that follows from that first step is—a new story, a meta-story about the past.

POLITICAL RECONCILIATION AND THE LANGUAGE OF HUMAN RELATIONS

By introducing "reconciliation" in the political arena, the political language has been added with yet another concept with a direct reference to human experience. States "trust" each other and have "friendly" relations and if necessary they even "apologize" or "express condolences" on behalf of their populations when other countries are suffering from, for instance, an earthquake. The more a state is regarded as a moral subject, the more we will see of a language that directly connects to other moral subjects'—such as individuals'—use of such concepts. This is a development away from the common view developed after the Second World War, that a state was an a-moral entity, that foreign policy was without moral dimensions, but based on interest beyond human moral categories.

The development of human rights, from the Universal Declaration of Human Rights, and subsequent conventions and resolutions, has brought the individual gradually into the realm of political relevance—not only as a rights-holder within each state but as subject to duties on behalf of the global community of states, in situations of war crimes and crimes against humanity through the principle of Responsibility to Protect.

While this is an international development, there is also an internal process in many states where indigenous populations have been recognized for what they are: pre-state inhabitants, societies, and cultures, living under depressing conditions in many states.

These two processes work independently, but they put the individual person, local communities and the strength and rights of non-state actors in focus. This makes it necessary for the state to adopt a language relevant for this change—necessary if it should be able to communicate and relate to these new actors and their conditions. As we have noted, in 2008, the historic injustices that the indigenous populations of Canada and Australia have been exposed to, were addressed by the governments of the respective countries in major acts of apology and an asking for forgiveness.

POLITICAL RECONCILIATION—A CONTRIBUTION TO POLITICS?
THE LACKING DIMENSION IN CONFLICT SETTLEMENT

The settlement of social conflict has for long been analyzed in terms of "conflict resolution," "conflict management" as well as "conflict transformation." Different schools have developed different approaches and preferences. Conflict resolution was in its early days accused of being naive or idealistic, since conflicts "could never be resolved," they were seen as energy which appears in different forms but never disappears—they can only be managed, since fundamental interests between people, including identities, were always at hand. Conflict management became the solution to the problem, meaning that the behavior of conflict actors can be "managed," controlled.

The parliament was a good example of this thinking: its members have learned how to behave, but were at the same time asked to maintain their views and not resolve the conflict between the parties over who should rule the country. Taking this argument one step forward is to say that the commitment and energy that there is among parties in conflict can actually be used to transform their inner and outer life conditions, and thereby transform the conflict as well. It can not only be expressed in different terms, or less violent ways, but used to reshape the situation in its totality. By incorporating or excluding new resources, new actors and concepts, this creates change both in real life and in the language about real life.

These three approaches do not explicitly take on the mental/attitudinal, dimension of conflict, but tend to focus on the issue(s) at stake—the incompatibility—and the conflict behavior. Again, the attitudes of parties are secondary to the analysis and practice of these concepts.

Democracy is a way of dealing with issues at stake. Peaceful cooperation and procedures of mutual respect in national and international relations are means by which conflict behavior can be made irrelevant. Reconciliation—if designed so as to fit a political context, is a concept which can indicate a process of dealing with the third corner of the triangle, that is, dealing with changing attitude, developing other mental images of the other. In this way, political reconciliation can serve both as a means and a goal, in the same way as democracy is a means for managing political issues, and a goal in itself—as long as we don't prefer another system for political decision-making.

It should also be said in this context, that what political reconciliation *is not,* is as important as what *it is*. For instance, it is not conflict resolution and it is not conflict management. Instead it is conflict reparation—through

RECONCILIATION AS POLITICS

a mechanism of recognition of the other side. A sloppy usage of reconciliation which equalizes the concept with conflict resolution doesn't benefit anyone, and contains a risk of smoothing out tension and real conflict issues. This is so since "reconciling" has an aura of overlooking and disregarding serious issues. Many a politician may like to use the concept so as to make the road to peace less bumpy.

To conclude and to be specific, the lacking dimension of conflict settlement may very well be represented by the political reconciliation concept. It has definitively put itself on the arena for judgment, and a long-term application and development of the concept will show how useful it is in the end.

WILL EVERYTHING BE FINE?

Political reconciliation never becomes more than—political. It is not a panacea for solving any civil conflict or tensions or injustices between families or neighbors. Such conflicts, however, often emerge in the wake of a peace agreement. While the effect of political reconciliation may very well be a relaxation of tension, both between individuals and community groups, there is always a large amount of issues and of violence—more or less related to the political conflict—which tend to return when stability and peace is at hand. Such conflicts may concern land issues, inheritance matters, old business relations, or family matters pending a settlement.

It is important to see, that political reconciliation is a tool for the long-term process—maybe sometimes inter-generational. It takes on a life of its own, when it has left its initial institutionalized forms of commissions, reparation measures, and renewed and explored relations. Therefore, such a process is not the perfect process to be controlled, or used, by anyone particular. If so, political reconciliation has a chance to fulfill its inbuilt expectation—to repair and to heal.

Appendix

Examples of Truth Commissions

Country	Installed	Period Analyzed	Report
Bolivia	1982	1967–1982	Dissolved Commission

Between 1964 and 1982 Bolivia was governed by a number of military juntas, beginning with the overthrow of President Estenssoro in 1964. A large number of disappearances and increasingly serious violations of basic human rights followed in the years to come in that period, and the following a presidential election in 1982 the National Commission of Inquiry Into Disappearances was established. Although dissolved, the two-year work of the Commission led to a number of trials.

Uganda I	1974	1971–1974	1974

The Ugandan President Idi Amin established during his rule a truth commission for inquiry into disappearances during his rule. The commission identified cases of disappearances for which the Public Security Unit and National Investigation bureau bore responsibility. (After having presented the report, the commissioners were targeted by the state in reprisal of their work.)

Appendix: Examples of Truth Commissions

Country	Installed	Period Analyzed	Report
Argentina	1983	1976–1983	1985

A military junta took over Argentina in 1976, while at the same time oppressing opposition through disappearances, torture, and killings. In 1983 the military government had to relinquish power following economic problems, the defeat in the Falkland/Malvinas war the year before, and international pressure. Elected President Raúl Alfonsín installed the National Commission on the Disappearance of Persons shortly after taking office and repealed a self-proclaimed amnesty for military officers.

Zimbabwe	1983	1983	No

Widespread violence against civilians in connection to the conflicts 1981–1983, between Ndebele people's opposition to President Mugabe's rule (basically Zimbabwe People's Revolutionary Army vs. Zimbabwe African National Liberation Army), were investigated by a commission set up by the President. Its report was never published.

Uganda II	1986	1962–1986	1994

The periods of rule under Idi Amin (1971–1979) and Milton Obote (1980–1985) in Uganda resulted in large numbers of killings and disappearances. After taking over power, already in 1986, President Museveni installed in 2009 a truth commission covering the periods of the two previous dictators.

Chile	1990	1973–1990	1991

From 1973 to 1989, beginning with the military take over of government by general Pinochet, Chile was in military hands. In 1989, General Pinochet accepted to hold national elections and was narrowly defeated by Patricio Aylwin, who set up the National Commission for Truth and Reconciliation.

APPENDIX: EXAMPLES OF TRUTH COMMISSIONS

Country	Installed	Period Analyzed	Report
Chad	1990	1982–1990	1992

The 1979 Lagos Accord lasted to 1981 when the forces of the then president and defense minister, respectively, began fighting over control of government. Defense minister Hissene Habré took control, initiated widespread repression, and was forced to leave the country in 1990. The year after, a truth commission was set up to investigate his period of rule. Hissene Habré was in May 2016 sentenced to life, on the basis of charges of crimes against humanity, war crimes, and torture.

El Salvador	1991	1980–1991	1993

The civil war in El Salvador had been going on for decades, including with military governments in power, and ended with the help of the UN in 1992. It was then agreed to set up a truth commission covering the period from the 1980s up to the end of the war.

Germany	1992	1949–1989	1994

Following the fall of the Berlin Wall and the dissolution of the German Democratic Republic, the German parliament set up The Study Commission for Working Through the History and the Consequences of the policies and practices of the German Democratic Republic, investigating human rights abuses by the government from 1949 to 1989.

Haiti	1994	1991–1994	1996

The overthrow of President Aristide in 1991 was followed by human rights abuses by the military regime that staged the coup. Aristide was reinstalled in 1993, with international backing, and a commission was established in 1994.

Appendix: Examples of Truth Commissions

Country	Installed	Period Analyzed	Report
Guatemala	1994	1962–1996	1999

The peace on paper for Guatemala arrived in 1996, after at least four decades of state repression, human rights abuses, and guerilla groups fighting the national army. Two years before, in 1994, the Commission for Historical Clarification was set up as part of the peace process.

Burundi	1995	1993–1995	1996

The killing of Burundi's first elected President Ndadaye in 1993 led to widespread violence. A UN commission was set up in 1995, working a year and handing over its final report in 2002.

South Africa	1995	1960–1994	1998

The process of ending the Apartheid system of South Africa—emerging as a legal structure in the 1940s—was initiated in 1990 and went on for about three years. Following elections and an interim constitution, a truth and reconciliation commission was established in 1995 for the purpose of investigating violations and, when appropriate, granting amnesty in exchange for information from the perpetrator.

Ecuador I	1996	1979–1996	Dissolved

A truth and justice commission investigating cases of human rights abuses in Ecuador between 1979 and 1996 was set up but had to close its work already in 1997. The background was a growing number of cases of paramilitary groups acting with impunity after serious human rights abuses in the countryside.

Rwanda	1999	1990–1992	1993

The genocide of Rwanda in 1994 took place after a civil war that started in 1990 and ended with a ceasefire in 1992 and a peace agreement in 1993 (Arusha Accords). This agreement could not hold back preparations for the genocide in spring 1994. The truth commission—named National Unity and Reconciliation Commission—was entrusted with investigating events beginning from 1992. It is now a permanent Rwandan institution.

APPENDIX: EXAMPLES OF TRUTH COMMISSIONS

Country	Installed	Period Analyzed	Report
Nigeria	1999	1966–1999	2005

While Nigeria has a long record of internal violence and human rights abuses, a short period of this history became the mandate of a truth commission established in 1999, to investigate the period in this respect from 1994 to 1999.

Country	Installed	Period Analyzed	Report
Uruguay	2000	1973–1985	1985

The Uruguayan political life was not void of political violence and at times truth commissions have been established when democratic leaders have found it possible to do so. In 1985 two commissions were set up (one on disappearances and one on the kidnapping and killing of two members of Parliament). These commissions had limited mandates and in 2000 a new truth commission was set up in order to investigate further disappearances in the period 1973 to 1985.

Country	Installed	Period Analyzed	Report
South Korea I	2000	2000–2004	2004

The change into democratic government in South Korea through the election of Kim Dae-Jung made it possible to investigate "Suspicious Deaths" during previous periods of military government. Since 1961 South Korea has had a military government up to 1987 when democracy was reinstated. Dae-Jung's presidential truth commission began its work in 2000.

Country	Installed	Period Analyzed	Report
Perú	2001	1980–2000	2003

As for many Latin American countries in the 1980s, also Perú saw a leftist guerilla group, the Sendero Luminoso. The capture of its leader, Abimael Guzman, and the forced ending of President Fujimori's term in 2000 and truth commission was installed in 2001 with the mandate to investigate the period of 1980–2000.

Appendix: Examples of Truth Commissions

Country	Installed	Period Analyzed	Report
Panama	2001	1968–1989	2002

The two generals Torrijos and Noriega were at the time well-known dictators of Panama. Their human rights abuses were systematic. In 2001, a truth commission was established with the mandate to investigate the years of their reign—1968–1989.

Yugoslavia	2002	1980-2000	

In the wake of the break-up of Yugoslavia, Kosovo became a political unit that over time obtained independence with an Albanian majority population and a Serbian minority. The regional war ended in 1995 through the Dayton Accords, the Kosovo conflict ended in 1999 and the Serbian president Milošević was replaced by Vojislav Kostuniça. He decided to set up a truth commission investigating was crimes in Slovenia, Croatia, Bosnia, and Kosovo—the former Yugoslav republics. The commission could not fulfill its mandate due to internal disagreements. It was internationally seen as a partial, pro-Serbian institution.

Timor Leste	2001	1974–1999	2005

Timor Leste experienced a few weeks of intense violence, destruction and looting in 1999, following a clear vote for independence in a UN referendum over its final status. Indonesian-supported militia groups were quelled only when international peacekeepers (Interfet) secured the country. The UN mission UNTAET established a truth commission as well as a serious crimes unit.

Sierra Leone	2002	1991–1999	2004

The internal war in Sierra Leone had several actors and some practiced serious violations of human rights, including mutilations, rape, and child soldier recruitment. The 1999 peace agreement between the government and the Revolutionary United Front included the establishment of a truth commission, which was established in 2000.

APPENDIX: EXAMPLES OF TRUTH COMMISSIONS

Country	Installed	Period Analyzed	Report
Ghana	2002	1966–2001	Partial reports

Since independence in 1957, Ghana had its first democratic transition of power not until 2001 when the then elected President Kufuor installed a truth commission entrusted with investigating human rights abuses in the past.

Democratic Republic of Congo	2003	1960–2002	2007

The truth commission was set up in connection to the 2002 comprehensive peace agreement, and was mandated to investigate political, societal and economic conflicts since the independence in 1960 up to 2002/2003. Names like Mobutu, Tchombe, Laurent Kabila, and his son Joseph Kabila, all reflect periods of violence and internal strife, conflict which over the years have cause the death of far beyond a hundred thousand persons.

Paraguay	2003	1954–1989	2008

Paraguay was during Stroessner's thirty-four-year-long military dictatorship one of the most consistently repressive regimes in Latin America. As democracy also gradually came back after 1989, a truth commission was established in 2003.

Morocco	2004	1956–1999	2005

Since independence, Moroccan political life has included secret detentions, disappearances and arbitrary arrests, practices which in periods have led to protests and pressure for clarifications. In 2004, king Mohammad VI established the Equity and Reconciliation Commission for dealing with forced disappearances, and arbitrary detentions in the period 1956–1999.

APPENDIX: EXAMPLES OF TRUTH COMMISSIONS

Country	Installed	Period Analyzed	Report
South Korea II	2005	2005–2010	2010

The 2004 report from the truth commission of 2000 was regarded as insufficient at the time of its presentation, and a new commission was established in 2005 (finalized its work in 2010) in order to shed light on human rights violations beginning with Japanese rule over Korea and ending with the end of the period with military governments.

Country	Installed	Period Analyzed	Report
Indonesia-Timor Leste	2005	1999	2008

Indonesia and Timor Leste initiated the first modern bi-lateral (interstate) truth commission by setting up the Commission for Truth and Friendship, entrusted with investigating events before and after the referendum in East Timor 1999. The Commission was set up by commissioners from both countries. In a statement by the Indonesian President Susilo Bambang Yodhoyono, systematic human rights violations of its military during occupation were officially recognized for the first time.

Country	Installed	Period Analyzed	Report
Liberia	2006	1979–2003	2009

The civil war of Liberia, beginning in 1989, claimed some 200,000 lives and a million persons displaced. Following interventions by the Economic Community of West African States a series of peace agreements were negotiated, ending with the 2004 Accra agreement. A truth commission was set up in 2005.

Country	Installed	Period Analyzed	Report
Ecuador II	2007	1984–1988	2010

A second truth commission was set up in 2007 covering systematic and grave human rights abuses, particularly in the period from 1984 to 1988 but also in later periods as well but to a lesser extent.

APPENDIX: EXAMPLES OF TRUTH COMMISSIONS

Country	Installed	Period Analyzed	Report
Kenya	2008	1963–2008	No

The 2007 elections in Kenya released intergroup and electoral tension on a level not seen before and a number of investigative commissions were set up in the country, as one of many initiatives resulting from the intervention of an inter-African high-level panel. The truth commission was established in 2008.

Honduras	2009	2009	2011

Honduras has been plagued by internal violence, like its neighboring Central American states have, for decades and the ousting of President Zelaya in 2009 was not a unique event. Following diplomatic pressure and internal negotiations an agreement was signed later in the year. Following elections, the new president, Lobo Sosa, established a truth commission.

Mauritius	2009	1638–2009	2011

The island state of Mauritius, south of the Indian continent, was colonized in the 1600s. Its economy has since then been gaining significantly from the import of workers—men, women, children—from India who have been treated as slaves in the agricultural industry mainly. To examine this practice and its consequences a truth commission was established in 2009.

Solomon Islands	2009	1999–2004	2012

Following a civil war in Solomon Islands between settlers and indigenous groups in the end of the 1990s, a peace agreement was signed in 2000. It could however not stop the parties from continued fighting, and a regional assistance mission, led by Australia, was set up in 2003 to restore local order.

APPENDIX: EXAMPLES OF TRUTH COMMISSIONS

Country	Installed	Period Analyzed	Report
Sri Lanka	2010	2002	2011

While several minor truth commissions have been working in Sri Lanka, the 2010 Lessons Learnt and Reconciliation Commission is the broadest since its limited mandate—to deal with events explaining the break of a cease-fire in 2002, and promote national unity—came in a period when the civil war between the Tamil Tigers (LTTE) and the government had ended, thus the commission came to represent a larger scope of issues than intended, along with higher expectations than was probably intended as well.

Country	Installed	Period Analyzed	Report
Brazil	2011	1946–1988	2014

The many military governments in Brazil from the 1940s and up to the end of the 1980s led to forced disappearances, killings, and other human rights violations in line with a practice during that period which also many other military regimes in the region applied. In Brazil, however, less persons were affected, generally speaking, than in neighboring countries, but the crimes could be the same. A truth commission set up in 2011 delivered its report on these violations, in 2014.

Country	Installed	Period Analyzed	Report
Nepal	2015	1996–2006	Ongoing

The armed conflict between the government and a Maoist guerilla from 1996 to 2006 caused serious violations of human rights in Nepal. The commission should investigate these, as well as develop compensation proposals for victims, and promote reconciliation.

Bibliography

Abu-Nimer, Mohammed, ed. *Reconciliation, Justice, and Coexistence: Theory and Practice*. Lanham, MD: Lexington, 2001.
Bell, Christine. *Peace Agreements and Human Rights*. Oxford: Oxford University Press, 2000.
Colmenares Olívar, Ricardo. *Los Derechos de los Pueblos Indígenas*. Caracas: Editorial Jurídica Venezolana, 2001.
Coser, Lewis A. *The Functions of Social Conflict*. Glencoe, IL: The Free Press, 1956.
Digeser, Peter E. *Political Forgiveness*. Ithaca, NY: Cornell University Press, 2001.
Donnelly, Jack. *International Human Rights*. Boulder, CO: Westview, 2012.
Dunn, James. *East Timor: A Rough Passage to Independence*. Double Bay, Aus.: Longueville, 2003
Feher, Michael. "Terms of Reconciliation." In *Human Rights in Political Transition: Gettysburg to Bosnia*, edited by Carla Hesse, and Robert Post, 325–28. New York: Zone, 1999.
Galtung, Johan. "Conflict as a Way of Life." *Essays in Peace Research* 3 (1969) 484–507.
Guterres, Francisco. "Elites and Prospects for Democracy in East Timor." PhD diss., Griffiths University, 2006.
———. *Reconciliaton in East Timor: Building Peace and Stability*. Stockholm: Swedish International Development Agency, Mimeo, 2003.
Humphrey, Michael. *The Politics of Atrocity and Reconciliation: From Terror To Trauma*. New York: Routledge, 2002.
Huyse, Luc, "Offenders." In *Reconciliation after Violent Conflict: A Handbook*, edited by David Bloomfield et al., 67–76. Stockholm: IDEA, 2003.
Ishizuka, Katsumi. *The Impact of UN Peace-building Efforts on the Justice System of Timor-Leste: Western versus Traditional Cultures*. Afrasian Center for Peace and Development Studies. Shiga: Ryukoku University, 2009.
Malley-Morrison, Kathleen, Andrea Mercurio, and Gabriel Twose, eds. *International Handbook of Peace and Reconciliation*. New York: Springer, 2013.
Nevins, Joseph. *A Not-So-Distant Horror: Mass Violence in East Timor*. Ithaca: Cornell University Press, 2005.
Nordquist, Kjell-Åke, and Kees Koonings. *Peace Process, Paramilitary CDDR and (International Support for) the MAPP/OEA Verification and Support Mission in Colombia*. Bogotá: Embassy of Sweden, 2005.
Orozco Abad, Iván. *Sobre los límites de la Conciencia Humanitaria. Dilemas de la Paz y la Justicia en América Latina*. Bogotá: Universidad de los Nades—CESO, 2005.
Pettersson, Therése, and Peter Wallensteen. "Armed Conflicts, 1946–2014." *Journal of Peace Research* 52/4 (2015) 536–50.

Bibliography

Philpott, Daniel. "An Ethic of Political Reconciliation." *Ethics and International Affairs* 23 (2009) 389–407.

———. *Just and Unjust Peace.* Oxford: Oxford University Press, 2012.

Said, Abdul Aziz, and Charles O. Lerche. "Peace as a Human Right: Toward and Integrated Understanding." In *Human Rights and Conflict: Exploring the Links Between Rights, Law, and Peace-Building*, edited by Julie A. Mertus, and Jeffrey W. Helsing, 129–49. Washington, DC: United States Institute of Peace, 2006.

Schaap, Andrew. *Political Reconciliation.* Routledge: New York, 2005.

———. "Political Reconciliation Through a Struggle for Recognition?" *Social and Legal Studies* 13/4 (2004) 523–40.

Shriver, Donald W., Jr. *An Ethic for Enemies: Forgiveness in Politics.* New York: Oxford University Press, 1995.

Teitel, Ruti G. *Transitional Justice.* New York: Oxford University Press, 2000.

Thompson, Janna. *Taking Responsibility for the Past: Reparation and Historical Justice.* Cambridge: Polity, 2002.

Tutu, Desmond. *No Future Without Forgiveness.* New York: Image, 2000.

United Nations. *An Agenda for Peace: Preventive Diplomacy, Peacemaking and Peace-Keeping: Report of the Secretary-General.* UN doc. A/47/277. June 17, 1992.

———. *Guidance Note of the Secretary-General: United Nations Approach to Transitional Justice.* United Nations, 2010.

———. *Report of the Secretary-General on the Protection of Civilians in Armed Conflict.* S/2001/331. March 30, 2001.

Uprimny, Rodrigo, ed. *¿Justicia transicional sin transición? Verdad, justicia y reparación para Colombia.* Bogotá: Centro de Estudios de Derecha, Justicia y Sociedad, 2006.

Walsh, Pat. *East Timor Political Parties.* Canberra: Australian Council for Overseas Aid, 2001

Yinan, He. "Overcoming Shadows of the Past: Post-Conflict Interstate Reconciliation in East Asia and Europe." PhD diss., Massachusetts Institute of Technology, 2004.

Zalaquett, José. "Confronting Human Rights Violations Committed by Former Governments: Principles Applicable and Political Constraints." In *Transitional Justice*, edited by Neil J. Kritz, 3–31. Washington, DC: United States Institute of Peace, 1995.

www.ingramcontent.com/pod-product-compliance
Lightning Source LLC
Chambersburg PA
CBHW050819160426
43192CB00010B/1817